Made in the USA
Lexington, KY
05 November 2019

# Table of Contents

# Chapter 5 - Website: Creating the Hub of Your Brand's Storytelling Universe......83

# Chapter 6 - Direct Marketing: Enchanting Customers by Speaking Only to Them .... 101

# Chapter 7 - Social Media: Nurturing a Dialog With Consumers Who Love You........................................119

# Conclusion - The Tip of the Brand Ecosystem Iceberg.....................................133

# Notes.....................................................137

# Index .....................................................149

# Praise For Beloved & Dominant Brands

"This quick-hitting, strategic brand read offers insights that many caretakers of their brands should find invaluable. From the focus on "why" to the "30-10-3" view to the introspective "competitive audit," this book offers a branding world through David's incisive lens."
– Ken Sadowski, The Beverage Whisper

"David is highly respected and smart, and has worked with some great brands. A good read for brands wanting to break-out."
– Jeff Klineman, Editor-in-Chief, BevNet.com

"A simple guide for anyone who wants to build brands people love."
– Nasahn Sheppard, Head of Global Customer Experience Design (CXD), Amazon Devices at Amazon

"It almost sounds like he practically knows what he might be talking about. Seriously, when someone has been involved with as many successful brands as David Lemley, you need to read the book."
– John Craven, CEO / Founder of BevNET, NOSH & Brewbound

"Brands are everywhere. We all have one whether we realize it or not. Understanding what they are, where they come from, and how to make them clear and compelling to a team and the market is the key to a sustainable competitive edge. Anyone interested in sharpening the focus of their brand will benefit from Mr. Lemley's insights and systems thinking in this book."
– Dennis Madsen, CEO, REI (retired)

"This book is a must-read not only for entrepreneurs but for any Retailer who is focused on creating their own Brand! David nails the essences of Brand Building from the first chapter, Turning Buyers into Believers!!! He speaks to reaching the soul of the consumer in every chapter!"
– John Yamin, Founder/Partner Sancus Partners and (former) CEO, Aryzta North America/LaBrea Bakery

# Acknowledgments

To all the individuals I have had the opportunity to lead, be led by, and stand next to while you changed the world for the better, thank you for being the inspiration and foundation for *Beloved & Dominant Brands*.

Without the experiences and support from my peers and teams at Retail Voodoo and Lemley Design, this book would not exist. All of you were more important than you could ever imagine – I heard every word of encouragement, coaching, and correction. And, believing that a career is like Harold Ramus's movie *Groundhog Day*, I stand before you blessed, with this book in hand and ready to catch the kid falling from a tree.

A special shout of gratitude to Slim Shady, Yuri Shvets, Brian Pieratt, Chris Cobb, Kiki Temkin Ariss, and Andrew Rubinstein for helping me show up on the in between days.

Having an idea and turning it into a book is as hard as it sounds. The experience is both internally challenging and rewarding. I especially want to thank the individuals that helped make this happen.

Blair Enns for teaching me the value of narrowly focused expertise, and to David C. Baker for being so frigging mean when telling me to "write the damn book already."

Thanks and love to Kat Simpson, Kelly Frazier, and Oscar Lemley for your tireless enthusiasm, questioning of my questions, and pushing this book to be "good and done." And to Bryn Mooth, for being a ferocious co-conspirator, tag-team wrestler, and interviewer extraordinaire. I trust, honor, and respect that you write for food.

Thank you to my lovely and outspoken wife, Diana, without whom none of the above would be true.

I want to thank God most of all, because without God I would be living in a van down by the river.

# Preface

In the past seven years, we've seen an explosion of better-for-you brands seeking to capture the attention of purpose-minded millennial consumers. And that's a good thing. The world needs more companies devoted to environmental sustainability, transparency in sourcing, clean ingredients, fair wages, and ethical practices.

But there comes a point in the better-for-you (BFY) brand's life cycle where good isn't enough. The founder-owner's passion isn't enough. Special ingredients aren't enough. Where the brand has gone from one of a kind to one of many.

I've dedicated my career to helping BFY brands and their leadership teams at those critical points. My team at Retail Voodoo are true believers on a quest to help BFY brands change the world for the better.

When I got into the design field 30-some years ago, brand strategy wasn't a thing. Design and marketing at the time was all about making cool stuff; sure, there was some strategy involved, but nobody talked about capital-B Branding.

As a young designer, I was in a position to create products and brands that were globally recognized and became part of pop culture — like Liz Claiborne's Curve fragrance, Nintendo's Legend of Zelda, and Starbucks in its earliest days. But doing amazing design work was not enough for me.

I wanted to ensure financial success for the clients I served. I recognized that there was a gap between what I knew and what companies needed from me. So I became a student: I learned in the real world and constantly educated myself. I've gone back to the University of Washington twice in my career. I refused to stop learning. The financial performance of the initiatives I worked on made me realize that there could be a formula to this work. And I was determined to crack the code.

## My Inspiration: The Seven Musts of Marketing

In 2013, as part of my ongoing quest for insights into business, marketing, and consumer behavior, I attended Tony Robbins's Business Mastery seminar. And that's where I experienced an a-ha moment: I heard about marketing guru Chet Holmes and his Seven Musts of Marketing. Holmes essentially applied systems thinking and insights into human behavior to the sales process, and his Seven Musts codified how to sell anything. His landmark book, "The Ultimate Sales Machine," which first presented the Seven Musts, was published in 2007. When I first heard about them in 2013, they resonated — and they still do today.

## Chet Holmes's Seven Musts of Marketing

1. Personal Contact
2. Direct Mail
3. The Internet
4. Company Brochures
5. Advertising
6. Public Relations
7. Customer Education

But while Holmes's Seven Musts were thoroughly practical for business-to-business (B2B) selling, I wanted to apply some of the same ideas to the brand-consumer relationship. Our BFY clients live in a landscape of rapidly changing consumer wants and behaviors, and some of Holmes's ideas seemed less adaptive to this market.

I'm an avid process hacker, and so I found myself hacking Holmes's Seven Musts, looking for ways to gain new insights, to move more quickly, to get it right the first time, and to help brands create sustained competitive advantage. I used them on my own business and found them to be powerful, universal truths of marketing. I began to implement them into our work for BFY brands as a competitive benchmarking tool.

Over time, we have evolved this thinking into our Brand Ecosystem model, a pyramid of seven marketing essentials that reveals brand strategy opportunities. The Brand Ecosystem guides all of our client engagements and provides a framework for evaluating a brand's position in the marketplace and charting its path toward Beloved & Dominant status in its category.

## The Passion Is Personal

Like many company founders in this space, my BFY conversion is deeply personal: I have a child who had food allergies at a young age, and cleaning up his diet resolved his issues. At the same time, my parents' generation started dying of cancer. The connections between food and health is part of our zeitgeist now, but in the 1990s, we didn't really believe the phrase we'd heard so often: You are what you eat.

I'm a BFY consumer and avid biohacker myself, always in search of the most optimized products that can help me feel and perform at my peak. And that's what led me to focus my energies on BFY brands.

I pivoted my company in 2011, renaming it after our process designed to help brands succeed in the retail environment. We reached out to all the pirates who would change the food system — those small companies led by visionary founders who are devoted to creating products that are better for the world. People told us we were crazy to focus on small brands, but we knew that consumer culture and the business world would catch up, eventually.

## Why This Book?

BFY brands matter. They're the pioneers. They're the ones with the innovation and passion and culinary chops to actually be on the ground making the change happen. By helping people with the BFY mindset find success, we've helped organize and mainstream the organic category. We've helped introduce clean food to a broader audience beyond crunchy-granola types. We've helped revolutionize agriculture. Our mission to reinvent the food system has virtually been accomplished. Kroger has natural and organic products in every aisle — that's the proof.

And now we're out to make sure these mission-driven brands attract legions of fans and outperform their competition. We call that Beloved & Dominant status.

I've written this book because I believe every brand leader should have access to the tools I'm sharing here. Every founder-owner, investor, Chief Marketing Officer (CMO), and entrepreneur who has a bold idea for reshaping the world for the better needs to back that idea up with proven business strategies. BFY consumers are different: they have higher standards, demands, and expectations. And in this book you'll find battle-tested strategies for reaching and convincing those consumers.

# Preface

My hope is that the generation behind me doesn't die of the same diseases that my siblings and my mom did. That's why I do this.

# Introduction

# The Life Cycle of Better-For-You Brands

We recently met with a new client who was facing a lose-sleep-over-it kind of business challenge. The newly hired chief marketing officer for a better-for-you (BFY) brand, she was tasked with sparking growth in a brand that had stagnated. The company had swept into its category with a disruptive product that consumers loved, but competition quickly pounced. In spite of the founder's passion, the brand had strayed from its mission, disconnected from its fans, and faced discontinuation from retailers. Investors were sniffing opportunity, but the executive team knew they'd have to make radical changes in order to appeal to funders — let alone to stay afloat.

She's not alone. BFY brands have humbled many a seasoned marketing executive.

The BFY category is moving fast, and brands are struggling to keep pace. (For our discussion, the term "BFY brands" refers to consumer brands in food, beverage, skincare, wellness, and lifestyle categories that aim to benefit people, the planet, animals, workers, communities, and so on.) Consumer preferences shift with the wind, trends come and go in about 10 seconds, and social media is full of shiny things that attract consumers' attention before they move on to something else. Today it's CBD; tomorrow it'll be microalgae.

---

BFY brands = consumer brands in food, beverage, skincare, wellness, and lifestyle categories that aim to benefit people, planet, animals, workers, communities, etc.

---

What's more, investors and multinational companies find BFY brands increasingly appealing as consumers' appetite for better-for-you products increases. At the same time, the barrier to entry in the BFY space is such that an entrepreneur with a killer product idea — a kale chip or a naturopathic skincare cream — can launch a company with some luck, word of mouth, and a pretty Instagram feed.

Decades ago, technology rewrote the old business adage, "he who has the most gold wins," to "he who owns the factory wins." Today, anyone with a bit of capital can make anything and sell it anywhere (just look at Etsy).

The new truth is this: He who has the idea — the brand — wins.

## The Limitations of BFY Brand Leadership

Having a great idea — a killer product and a brand story to match — isn't enough. Yet we see executives in the BFY category operating as if their product and their mission were the only requisites for success.

And heads of marketing are buying into this "good is enough" business mindset, too. In the BFY space, marketing leadership is either stagnant or inexperienced with small, niche brands.

Better-for (people, planet, community, workers, animals) companies tend to attract three types of marketers:

- Entrepreneurs
- Investors
- Conventional marketing ideologists

And none of these types are expert at reinventing the tools of marketing to reveal new insights and generate results quickly.

Entrepreneurs — often company founders doubling as chief marketing officers — are filled with enthusiasm, running on the cult of their own personality and a combination of ambition, fear, and gut instinct. Their passion means they often conflate the company's brand with their own personal brand, and they can't separate the two to make tough decisions. They figured out how to hack the product, but they don't know enough to hack the systems of marketing as well.

Investors — drawn to the brand by the passionate owner — are great at data analysis, especially historical data. They want results and will bring in the expertise necessary to get them where they want to go. But these investors increasingly come from the tech world, not consumer goods, and they don't know the market. They can be skeptical, impatient, and suspicious of the outside experts they hire.

Conventional marketing ideologists — armed with MBAs and Consumer Packaged Goods experience — are really great at strategies and tactics that are tried, true, formulaic, and timeless. But they often don't understand how BFY brands differ from other brands they've worked on. They underestimate the hurdles that the founder-owner can erect. Because they don't understand other parts of the business, they're uncomfortable wearing the many hats required in a small, dynamic organization.

## The Life Cycle of a BFY Brand

No matter how experienced or well-intentioned their leadership teams, we see that BFY brands tend to follow a predictable trajectory.

Let's look at how a BFY food brand might evolve:

*figure I-1*

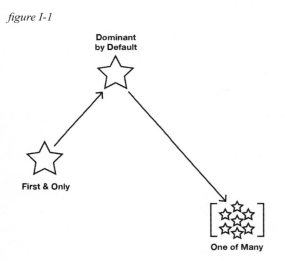

## First & Only

Inspired by a lifestyle, a dietary need, or a health issue, the visionary founder hacks a recipe to create a new product that meets his family's needs. Invariably, he hitches the product to a functional ingredient or way of eating that's a little on the fringe — like chia or CBD or keto. "You should make this into a business," his friends say. And so he does.

Thanks to a growing tribe of fans and backed by early-adopting retailers, Original Brand catches on. Fueled by the social media love of its base, the founder-owner may branch into regional grocery chains, if production capacity can keep up with demand. And that's a big if.

## Beloved by Default

Seeing Original Brand's success, another company, then another, enters the market with their own chia/CBD/keto products. Maybe they have a twist: more culinary flavors or more Instagram-friendly marketing tactics. Owing to its primacy in the market, the passion of its loyalists, and the uniqueness of its story, Original Brand continues to dominate the category by default. For awhile.

## One of Many

Seeking to capitalize on the popularity of chia/CBD/keto products, other players join the game. Retailers launch private label versions. Big Food companies create cheap knockoffs. Suddenly, Original Brand is relegated to the bottom shelf by store managers eager to promote the house- and big-brand products. In a market that's now saturated, Original Brand loses shares as customers choose based on price rather than based on brand narrative.

Original Brand's founder-owner and his first-generation leadership team remain anchored in First & Only mode, too biased by their own fandom to recognize the growing competition for the threat that it is. The marketing and sales teams are usually the first to wake up and smell the coffee. Social media campaigns no longer convert to dollars. Retail buyers grill the sales reps on slowing velocity and threaten to limit distribution. Consumers move on to whatever becomes the next chia/CBD/keto darling.

## Beloved & Dominant

There's a sweet spot in the BFY brand space. We call it Beloved & Dominant. These brands are:

- Embraced by passionate fans who love not just the quality products, but also what the brand stands for in the world
- Impervious to pricing and new product challenges from competitors
- Favored by retailers who see the brand's success as key to their own
- Widely talked about by major outlets, lifestyle influencers, and everyday users
- Attractive to larger companies seeking sources of innovation or to the right kind of investors

BFY brands across categories — natural beauty, nutritional supplement, beverage, wellness — follow the same trajectory: They catch fire, win early fans, then lose traction as lookalikes come into the market.

There is a return path from One of Many to Beloved & Dominant. It's potholed with difficult decisions. And it starts with the competitive audit.

*figure I-2*

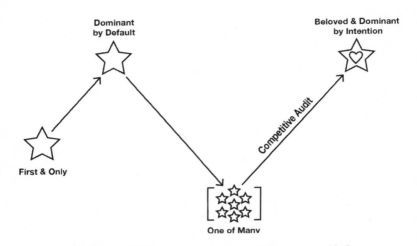

**Return to Dominance via the Competitive Audit**

Many BFY brands have adopted a "hacker mentality" — finding creative and clever ways to overcome problems. They hack nutrients, hack snacking, hack time, hack life, hack anything to get results for busy people. Imagine if you could apply this same hacker mentality to your brand's marketing — in a way that would return your brand to category dominance.

You can. And it starts with conducting a killer competitive audit that will illuminate a new strategy for your brand.

---

A competitive audit provides a realistic, unbiased assessment of your current state and your opportunities based upon competition, your company culture, and your brand's strengths and weaknesses. This analysis, combined with a deep understanding of the changing nature of consumer preferences, provides the platform on which brand strategy is built.

---

## When Marketers Distrust Research

Often, without realizing it, marketers manipulate outside data in an effort to validate what they already know, by writing questions or seeking answers that will confirm their cognitive bias. Marketing teams that have experienced some version of bias in the past are, therefore, reluctant to undertake this kind of deep research a competitive audit requires.

Occasionally, when my agency starts working with a client, she'll come to the table with an older competitive audit, one she's not especially happy with. One client complained that her previous agency had spent too much time and money on a report that wasn't at all insightful. "My high school daughter could have done that," she said.

We get it: There are plenty of pitfalls to category and competitive audits. Many research agencies limit their analysis to what they find online, creating a sort of sanitized view of packaging and branding. At retail, though, the visual landscape is a jungle, and the box or bag that looks great on a desktop monitor struggles to stand out in a sea of competitors on the shelf. Artwork for a print or outdoor ad campaign might look good in PowerPoint but very different on newsprint or a billboard.

Effective competitive research isn't an academic exercise. It looks at how the brand lives in the real world and benchmarks its competency.

## Category vs. Competitive Audit

Marketers often confuse or conflate the category audit with the competitive audit. Both are useful, and we often run them sequentially for our clients. But they're different beasts.

A category audit is limited to a single aisle. Let's say you're a bread bakery. A category audit examines the communication conventions for bread brands on the shelf. It looks at design and positioning trends among bakeries, comparing bread brands to one another.

We use category audit as first tool with our clients to bring data to what is often a subjective point of view. BFY brands often rely on emotion and perception to gauge the effectiveness of their marketing efforts: the number of likes the brand has on social media, raves from fans, or pats on the back from their ad agency when they run a cool campaign. Our category audit collects data about the brand and its competitive set at retail. Then we evaluate it strictly through the lens of the brand — which we define as the promises you make and the way you keep them.

---

Brand = the promises you make and the way you keep them

---

A competitive audit takes a wider and higher view to answer the question: What else is competing for the consumer's dollar? Considering a nutritional supplement, for example, a category audit looks at the shopper's entire life to identify what she might purchase instead of the supplement. If she's interested in self-care, she might buy an upscale skincare product instead, or make an appointment for a massage, or buy a juicer.

To call it a competitive audit is a bit of a misnomer: It isn't about your competition, it's about your brand. And it can help you see a bigger world than you currently perceive.

# A Framework Building Beloved & Dominant Brands

In conducting a competitive audit for our BFY clients, we use a series of seven critical marketing disciplines to benchmark our client's brand across its competitive landscape. These disciplines form what we call the Brand Ecosystem.

This process simplifies the communication strategy across multiple channels and streamlines the messaging into a cohesive, ownable narrative that delivers a brand's message to critical audiences.

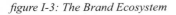
*figure I-3: The Brand Ecosystem*

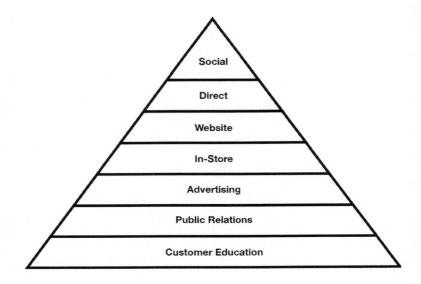

The pyramid-shaped Brand Ecosystem model helps everyone involved to see clearly how each of these marketing disciplines ladder into one another. The theory is simple: A strong foundation is the key to any structure (whether physical or abstract). Any outage in the system will cause the marketing hierarchy to tilt out of balance and collapse.

We ask a series of simple questions for each of the platforms in the ecosystem. The answers are then used against a rubric of what perfection could look like for each brand. We then compare all the communication musts a brand needs to compete effectively in its given category. When complete, we compile the answers into a version of the pyramid and benchmark our client and its competitive set within the context of those answers.

At a glance, marketers can see how the brand is performing, how they need to pivot investment to other channels, where opportunity lies. While the highest level of performance is indicated by solid outlines, more often the graphic looks like this, with the dotted lines showing outages:

*figure I-4: The Brand Ecosystem Unbalanced*

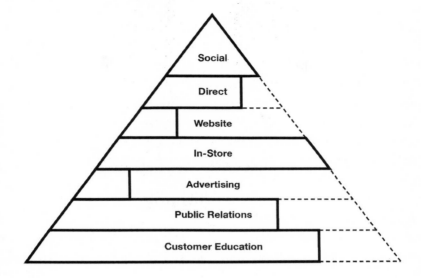

This Brand Ecosystem pyramid takes the conversation out of the realm of emotion, predisposition, and bias that most brand teams surround themselves with and into the realm of impartiality, reality, and fact. It doesn't disallow opinion and gut instinct, but it bases those inputs on a solid analytical framework.

The Brand Ecosystem creates engagement between brands and human beings. It builds brands that better-for-you consumers actively crave with their mind, body, and soul.

## How to Apply the Brand Ecosystem Model

Ready to advance your brand, elevate sales, build your audience, and achieve Beloved & Dominant status in your category? Tired of spinning your wheels with marketing initiatives that don't really move the needle?

# BELOVED & DOMINANT BRANDS

We're sharing the Brand Ecosystem with BFY marketing, entrepreneurs, C-suite leaders, Chief Marekting Officers (CMOs), and investors who are looking to ensure their brand plays a major role in reshaping the category landscape.

The following chapters lay out the Brand Ecosystem pyramid, with each chapter addressing a single marketing discipline. You'll discover ways to hack traditional marketing methods for your brand, along with practical examples from the real world that demonstrate what successful Beloved & Dominant brands do. We'll dig deeper into the why behind each must, unpacking it for BFY brands with insights designed to help bring clarity and purpose.

Entrepreneurs, investors, and CMOs can use each chapter to benchmark their own brands against their competitive set — performing their own high-level competitive audit. You will understand how to evaluate your brand through the lens of competition, divine a new brand strategy, and chart the path to making your brand powerful enough that competition, as you have known it until now, is irrelevant.

If you are an expert marketer, serial entrepreneur, investor, or the wolf they bring in to fix the brand, we hope you'll appreciate this book each time you thumb through its easy-to-read, plain-spoken advice.

Let's get started.

# Chapter 1

# Customer Education: Turning Buyers Into Believers

*figure 1-1: The Brand Ecosystem: Customer Education*

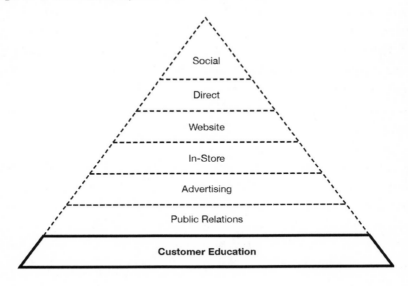

Take a look at packaging across the BFY space. It leans heavily on information with bits of copy about features, ingredients, and attributes:

- Free from high-fructose corn syrup, gluten, allergens, and all the other "baddies"
- Low-glycemic
- Plant-based
- Antioxidant-rich
- High-protein, high-fiber
- All-natural, organic, whole, vegan, pure

BFY brands leverage box- and bag-front copy to help consumers understand how the product benefits their wellbeing. As consumers get savvier about what they put in their mouths, they want to know what's in food and drinks, and how it will make them feel. And food marketers are responding, adding functional ingredients like antioxidants, prebiotics, plant extracts, omega-3s, and more. As processed food gets better for us, it can get a little more complicated.

If education is essential, then why are so many BFY brands going about it all wrong? They simply overload consumers with too much information about the products. In a crowded retail environment, TMI is not helpful.

Beloved & Dominant BFY brands understand that the purpose of customer education is not to sell them stuff; it's to create evangelists.

*"The bottom line is that every company in the world needs to prove that their products are necessary, rather than demanding that customers believe it to be so."* — William Craig, president of WebFX[1]

# Education as Part of the Traditional Customer Journey

Yes, you need to educate consumers about your features and attributes in order to convince them to buy. In fact, education is the first step of the traditional Customer Journey, the path that an individual traverses as she goes from curious to convinced to craving a brand with her mind, body, and soul.

*figure 1-2: Customer Journey Map*

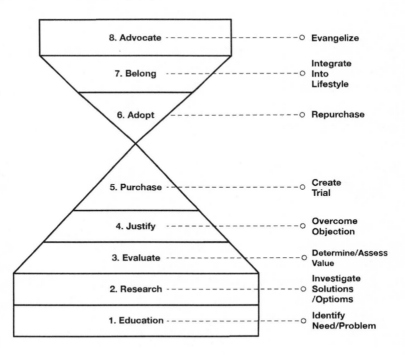

In the BFY category, the Customer Journey might look like this:

1.  Identify problem — I think I may be sensitive to gluten, or I'm interested in the keto diet, or I want to lose weight, or I want my family to eat healthier
2.  Research — I'll ask my friends, see what's trending on social media, and maybe browse the natural products at my grocery store or visit Whole Foods
3.  Evaluate — I'll pick up a product from the shelf or view an item online, or maybe consult my mobile phone while I'm out shopping
4.  Justify — I'll decide if what the brand is promising is worth the product's price
5.  Purchase — I'll take this to the checkout

And here's where the Customer Journey ends for the vast majority of BFY brands. Most marketers think their work ends when the consumer has made that first purchase.

But it doesn't. Not by a long shot.

If you don't fully educate the consumer, she'll never get to the last three steps. Let's take a look at the final parts of the Customer Journey:

6.  Adopt — I love this product, I love what it does for me, and my family loves it
7.  Belong — Not only do I love the product, but I admire what the brand stands for; I feel like I'm part of the tribe of others who support the brand too
8.  Advocate — I can't wait to tell everyone I know about how great the brand and its products are; I'm going to encourage

my friends to try them and post about the brand on social media

In these final three steps, the brand can capitalize on the true value of the customer. We know that it's less costly for companies to sell to existing customers than to recruit new ones.

# Retention Marketing vs. Acquisition Marketing

- Acquiring a new customer can cost 5x more than retaining an existing one
- Increasing customer retention by 5% can increase profits by more than 25%
- The success rate of selling to an existing customer is 60%–70%; it's 5%–20% for a new customer[2]

When you have advocates for your product or service, you have the best possible kind of customer. Your advocates are:

- Passionate, loyal, and thrilled to recommend you
- Champions when it matters; they are your public defenders when times are difficult; they assume your mistakes are honest
- Trusting. They believe you have their best interests at heart
- Hyper-repeat customers

When your brand creates a body of advocates, you can succeed in unimaginable ways.

# Customer Education as the Foundation for Marketing

In an era of eroding trust for brands and megachoice in nearly all categories, customer education forms the foundation of the

Brand Ecosystem. It plays to the other elements because without customer education, the pyramid would topple over.

## About Your Products

You may be thinking that customer education is only for companies with challenging products that solve complex, persistent problems. And you would be partially right.

As BFY brands add new ingredients like adaptogens and prebiotics, it's incumbent upon them to introduce shoppers to those unfamiliar ingredients and convey their benefits. This is also the place where you can make any complex or technical functionality easier to understand. Brands often make the mistake of drowning people in information to the point that consumers cannot hear or absorb what they're being told.

The opportunity to explain your technical details gets more meaningful when you clarify what your brand stands for and how you integrate your mission into your products.

## About Your Brand

Your brand — and the way that you talk about it — should be about so much more than your ingredients.

---

Your Brand = Your Promise + the Way You Keep It

---

Positioning your brand on features (ingredients) and benefits (flavor, nutrition) is riskier than ever, because trends come and go more quickly than ever. We live in a world where consumers are open to new ideas, where technology makes it easy for people to discover something and share it with others, and where social currency depends on being in the know.

Consumers need to understand your brand in the context of the real world. They want to know what problems your brand and product(s) will solve, what your process looks like, why you make your products, and where you stand on issues they care about.

Customer education is your opportunity to explain why you exist in the world beyond your products. It's the place to weave your purposes, your causes, and your beliefs behind the "why" your business exists beyond making a profit, into a narrative that invites them into your world. It's your brand's chance to get people to buy in to your mission and your vision of how you're going to improve the world.

---

"Very few people or companies can clearly articulate WHY they do WHAT they do. By WHY I mean your purpose, cause, or belief — WHY does your company exist? WHY do you get out of bed every morning? And WHY should anyone care? People don't buy WHAT you do; they buy WHY you do it." — Simon Sinek[2]

---

If there's a starting point when it comes to educating your customers, it's probably this: Believe in your product. But more than that, make sure you know how to express that belief.

Customer education focuses on equipping your customers with the skills and knowledge they need to successfully integrate your offering into their lives. It's a process of knowledge transfer that continues throughout customers' lifespans, providing value to them along the way and providing them a sense of co-authorship in your brand as they move from student to teacher in their own sphere of influence.

## Be the Right Kind of Educator

Perhaps you associate education with your own classroom experience: memorizing fractions and spelling words. Viewed through this lens, education feels like work, for both the giver and the receiver.

Instead, think of education as part of your overall consumer experience. In a seminal Harvard Business Review article titled "Welcome to the Experience Economy," speakers and management advisors Joe Pine and James Gilmore introduced the concept of the experience as a distinct business offering (like goods or services). In their book, "The Experience Economy," Pine and Gilmore write about ways to combine learning with other attributes or activities that make the lessons more "sticky" for consumers.

Consider the ways Pine and Gilmore proposed to wrap your consumer education efforts into other messaging:

- Edutainment = *Education + Entertainment (capturing and holding attention)*
- Eduscapist = *Education + Escapist (changing context)*
- Edusthetic = *Education + Esthetic (fostering appreciation)*[a]

In addition, a brand's persona, or archetype (see Chapter 5: Websites for more about the 12 Archetypes of a Brand) will dictate its approach to educating consumers. A "Jester" brand will make learning fun; an "Explorer" brand will create a sense of adventure and discovery.

# The Long-Term Benefits of Customer Education

Customer education is the easiest way to build trust and turn customers into advocates. Your aim should be not only to give them the information they need in order to choose you for that very first purchase, but also to carry your message to others.

When you educate your customers, you empower them:

- To advocate on your behalf (increasing likelihood for word-of-mouth referrals)
- To use your products with confidence
- To work independently within your brand's suite of products

But education isn't strictly limited to your external audience. Education empowers your sales team to have an established script that highlights points of parity and points of difference between your products and your competitors'. It empowers your retail partners to know where and how to place your products. It empowers your R&D team to innovate with confidence, guided by the brand's mission and beliefs.

# Consumer Education in Practice

Educating the customer about your brand's ethos and your products' performance is the heart of all communication efforts wrapped up in the discipline of marketing. It's the foundation of the Brand Ecosystem.

*figure 1-3: The Brand Ecosystem: Unbalanced*

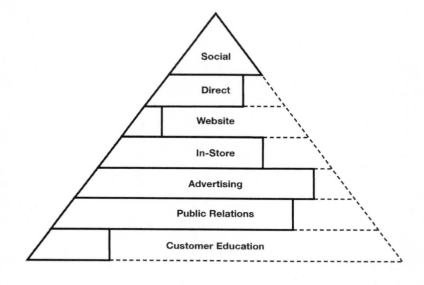

Customer education forms the core messaging for all other planks in the Brand Ecosystem pyramid model.

In the forthcoming chapters, we'll dig deeper into each of the Brand Ecosystem's communication platforms in print, online, and in the real world.

## The Ethos of a Brand

In our overcrowded, copy-cat marketplace, points of difference that are function- and feature-based are no longer sustainable. Consumers today are tuning out marketing and tuning in to those brands that represent shared values.

Clifford Geertz, dubbed the Godfather of Cultural Anthropology, put it something like this: Ethos and worldview describe how cultures create a seamless, unified system. The ethos (an understanding of how we should act in the world) is supported by the worldview (a picture of how the world really is), and vice versa. In a sense, ethos and worldview are what differentiate one culture from another. And it is the culture that traditionally gives individuals their definition of self—who they are, what they believe, and how they should act.

This ethos is what we call a brand's WHY. Why it exists, why it behaves the way it does, why it makes the products it makes. In other words, the promise that it makes and the way it keeps that promise.

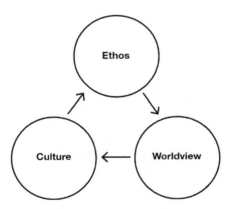

## Customer Education: Who's Doing It Well?

## Whole Foods
Whole Foods is essentially preaching to the converted; you wouldn't think the brand would have to do much educating. After all, shoppers come to Whole Foods specifically for the BFY products it sells.

Yet the brand invests heavily in education both online and in-store to enhance the customer experience and, most important, to drive trial and purchase of new products. Point-of-selection signage in different departments help shoppers choose: the right seafood (with information from the Monterey Bay Aquarium's Seafood Watch program on different types of fish), seasonal produce (with signage indicating local offerings), or a new kind of cheese.

Online, the company's "Whole Story" blog creates opportunity for information and conversation. For a food or retail brand, recipes and culinary tips are must-have content that helps consumers find new ways to use fresh and packaged food products. The blog spotlights new products (tip for BFY marketers: find ways to get your products highlighted here). And its lifestyle content includes entertaining ideas and recipes related to holidays, including, notably, Ramadan.

## Brooks

This athletic shoe company is all about the run. For 70-some years, the brand was sold exclusively at specialty running stores, where trained salespeople would help fit customers in the right shoes based on their running style and physiology.

When Brooks expanded into the big-box chain Dick's Sporting Goods, it was a great opportunity to grow sales. But brand leaders knew they wouldn't have experienced salespeople helping customers make the right choice. Brooks shoe boxes would have to handle the consumer education.

The marketing team boiled what was a 20-minute sales consultation down to a system of icons that would help a shopper match their needs with the right shoe. The power of this graphic system was not just that people could self-shop; it also educated Dick's frontline employees on how to select a running shoe. What started as Brooks's proprietary fitting system became a guide for the whole category; it democratized relevant information for any shopper and any shoe brand. Soon the idea of using iconography to fit shoes by running style/foot/need expanded across other brands and other retailers. Even specialty stores selling Brooks shoes started asking for the same kind of customer education system. This reflects a "brand as consultant" mode of communication; it demystified Brooks's underlying shoe technology so consumers could make smart choices.

## West Marine

West Marine is sort of the REI for the boating industry: a multistate chain of outfitters for sailors, boaters, anglers, and other watersport enthusiasts. West Marine doesn't sell boats, but rather all the rigging, gear, safety equipment, clothing, and other stuff boaters need.

Unfortunately, West Marine's long-standing brand vocabulary and communication strategy reflected the "crusty old salt" reputation of boating old-timers. The brand focused on safety and performance — certainly important aspects of boating products — but at the expense of one key fact: Boating is fun. The whole in-store experience was a downer, especially for female customers (and half the people on boats are women).

A shift of perspective — remembering that people go out on the water to have fun — changed the brand's whole vocabulary. It started to talk to customers as water-loving peers.

*figure 1-4: Example of The Facets of Brand Voice*

| | |
|---|---|
| **Our Voice and Tone is Simple.**<br>**Write Like a Boater Would Talk to a Boater** | |

West Marine is the Boating Community's most experienced outfitter and advisor. Four decades ago, we revolutionized the concept of chandlery by focusing on the quality of service and broad assortment. Today our continued passion for helping Boaters makes our stores the place to gather and learn as a commmunity, uplifting and outfitting those who share our obsession for The Boating Lifestyle. West Marine understands why you boat.

**There are three facets to our voice.**

| **Reflective** | **Directive** | **Supportive** |
|---|---|---|
| Used to build Brand through reinforcing our connection to the Community of Boaters through statements that underscore our passion for Boating. | e.g. West Advisor — giving our opinion on the best solution for whatever adventure they have in mind, from maintenance to sailing around the world. | This is where we share our expertise. We help Boaters get outfitted for any adventure they are planning, from cruising, sailing, and fishing to taking the grandkids out for an afternoon. |

As you're evaluating your brand's customer education efforts, look closely at tone of voice. Are you speaking to your audience in an authentic, on-brand way that they'll respond to?

# Educating Customers Is an Obvious Investment

Marketers who undervalue customer education think it's too expensive. They don't understand what's in it for the brand — and they may think that teaching consumers about the product and the brand gives people information they need to switch to a competitor.

When customer education is the foundation of communication, Beloved & Dominant brands move from guessing what consumers want to meeting needs they know well because they deeply understand the audience. Beloved & Dominant brands stop simply reacting to competitors' latest moves and instead lead via a virtuous cycle of optimizing their products.

Making it about them, in turn, delivers results for you.

## Your Competitive Audit: Customer Education

1.  How do you explain your brand's dramatic differences and similarities to other brands and products in your consumer's consideration set?

2.  How have you expressed the most compelling thing about your brand story? Your collective offering? Each individual product?

3.  How can you explain your brand beyond features and benefits in a way that overcomes price resistance?

4.  Have you told your origin story interwoven with the what, how, where, and why behind your brand?

5.  Is your brand language clear and concise?

6.  Is your brand's voice represented in your customer education? Does it sound like the category or does it help define the category?

7.  Have you removed the insider lingo from your brand's customer education platform?

# BELOVED & DOMINANT BRANDS

# Chapter 2

# PR: Building a Sphere of Authenticity

*figure 2-1*

## The Brand Ecosystem: PR

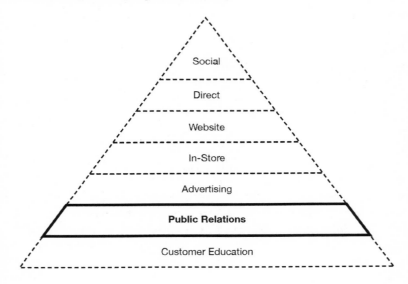

It used to be said: There's no bad PR.

But in the swirl of online commentary and a 24/7 news cycle that moves with lightning speed, there is bad PR. And the BFY category is not immune from negative news. Product recalls, culturally insensitive products or ad campaigns, and bogus health claims have all threatened brand reputations.

It used to be that the point of PR was to build fame. But for Beloved & Dominant BFY brands, PR is about way more than generating attention and buzz. PR is a long term, slow, and deliberate reputation management process that is designed to get your brand awareness mixed into the cocktail sauce of public opinion. It is not a once-and-done activity. Nor does it replace other sales and marketing tactics.

---

"A big part of how we're getting our message out and our narrative out is earned [media]." — Peter McGuinness[1]

---

Public relations sounds so easy. After all, it's really just placing stories and getting respected third parties to talk about you. But when viewed through the lens of brand building, PR is an integral foundation of all of the other planks in Brand Ecosystem pyramid.

Public relations allows for long-form storytelling, where third party experts can talk about your brand and your products in an unbiased way. For this reason, PR is a natural, logical extension of your customer education platform in a way that's distinct from social media. Without a customer education platform that contains a readily available, easily accessible baseline of information, journalists researching a story have no way to find or reach you.

A concentrated, focused PR campaign should be part of every brand launch or relaunch. Developing an advertising campaign, in-store experience, direct, and social program that includes a supporting PR arm is far more effective than one without.

---

PR is a natural, logical extension of your customer education platform in a way that's distinct from social media.

---

## PR Conveys a Brand's Authentic Purpose

When I asked Chris Olivier, an Atlanta-based CMO and private investor in emerging-stage food brands, about the role that modern PR can play, he agreed that it's a key part of an overall marketing program. *"PR is an antiquated term,"* he told me. *"Today, PR is an authenticity play. We could call it 'authenticity relations' instead of 'public relations' or 'media relations.' It needs a new name."*

In our conversation, Chris observed that the most important role of PR for BFY brands is to provide an unbiased point of view that reinforces a brand's authentic purpose. *"Consumers are smart and able to sniff out inauthenticity more quickly and easily than ever before,"* he told me.

*"PR is an opportunity to drive authenticity. One of many brands are scratching and clawing for differentiation and authenticity,*

*and only a select few survive. You need something to hang your hat on. Taste and ingredients are important, yes, but the consumer cares about the backstory more than ever and they are paying attention to every step the brand makes.*

*"It's not PR alone that gets you there, but everything you do from a branding perspective is more likely to get traction if you think about authenticity-building public relations as an integral part of your base program."*

Chris noted that affiliate links between media outlets (whether that's a popular blog, an Instagram influencer, or a let media outlet like Wirecutter.com) means that PR can be monetized. *"PR can be closed loop now,"* he told me. *"Now you can actually click and buy something. We are able to answer the question, 'What's my ROI on my PR efforts?' That was always difficult to prove; you could measure impressions, but what does that mean?"*

---

*"PR is an antiquated term. Today, PR is an authenticity play. We could call it 'authenticity relations' instead of 'public relations' or 'media relations'".* — Chris Olivier[2]

---

# 4 Essentials of PR for BFY Brands

## 1. PR Starts With Your Brand Story

How do you create naturally occurring (organic) evangelists for the brand? For people to swear by your brand, your story needs to be good. Really good. It must go far beyond just explaining the technical functionality of your products.

Consumers need to understand WHY your brand exists. They want to know what problems your brand and product(s) will solve, what your process looks like, why you make your products, and where you stand on issues they care about.

Your story is your WHY. Not everyone will respond to your why. Not everyone will like your brand, and that's OK. But your why needs to be so powerful and deeply embedded in your organization that you're willing to take a punch in defending it. Beloved & Dominant brands have a bold point of view, along with the audacity to say something that may not be popular with people who aren't in their tribe.

Earned media — editorial coverage generated by active outreach efforts on your brand's behalf — touches on emotional storytelling and human connection, and only then does it dig into functionality, features, and benefits. Yes, you can get into the nitty-gritty details of how your product meets a dietary need or your fitness water fuels better workouts. But media coverage needs to lead with a personal story. Otherwise, people won't care.

As Chris Olivier told me, "A brand's WHY has to be there from the first touchpoint. But the consumer must love the product before they care about the WHY. The brand's ethos has to dovetail with the quality of the product. The consumer doesn't want to get that level of detail until they've decided to move their chips in, and this gets back to why third party validation through PR is so important."

## 2. PR Can Especially Benefit BFY Brands With Functional Nutrition, Wellness Claims, or Other Technical Aspects

Food, beverage, and skincare products are all getting more technically complex; products in the BFY space incorporate functional ingredients designed for specific nutritional needs or wellness benefits. Adaptogens, phytonutrients, alkalization, aplha-lipoic acid — consumers need help understanding unfamiliar ingredients and their benefits.

When you have something that has a technical component to it or a complex benefit structure, getting third-party experts to speak to the benefits in a scientific, yet human, way can be highly effective. From food magazines to national newspapers to well-regarded bloggers, there's a host of digital and traditional media outlets covering BFY trends. Consumers look to trusted sources to help them decipher information related to diet and wellness.

All the medical of nutritional claims overtly expressed or implied will be met with the hint of skepticism if your story doesn't include, well, your story. Instead of pushing the nutritional education or science on the public, first get them comfortable with your origin story. Once they're intrigued, allow people to discover the science of your offering on their own.

If you insist on weaving science into everyday life, make it tangible. Don't tell your audience what happens in a laboratory (or worse, in a focus group). Instead, share with them how you used your product on a weekend trip with your family and friends.

## 3. PR is Integrated With, But Different From, Other Communication Channels

Bold BFY brands are employing a hybridized modern PR strategy to get their stories in front of new audiences. Yes, traditional PR that uses more conventional print and online media still exists. But the discipline is venturing into social media as well. PR agencies themselves are shifting focus from wooing journalists to reaching consumers wherever they are, whatever they read. PR today is a blend of branding, media, and consumer marketing.

As we mentioned above, media coverage allows for long-form narrative about your brand story. It builds credibility in a way that social media never could.

On the flip side, social media is cute, sexy, snackable, and quick. Leverage your social channels to point to online articles and to your customer education platform. Use social to leverage the heck out of whatever earned media you can generate.

---

*"Adding to the brand conversation, Chobani is running paid content with Time and Thrillist that it called "editorial collaborations" about the company and its people. Chobani is also adding content to its website, including stories showcasing some of its employees talking about what food means to them or what it means to work for Chobani."* — Chobani CMO[3]

---

PR, advertising (which we'll cover in the next chapter), and social media (Chapter 7) are interrelated but separate disciplines. They're all founded on customer education.

*figure 2-2*

# The Brand Ecosystem: Connected

# 4. Brands Can't Be Greedy About PR

BFY brands tend to be led by charismatic founder-owners whose devotion drives the business and unites the tribe. These people are often unapologetic outliers with strong points of view and passion worn proudly on their sleeves. Sometimes these evangelists make great brand ambassadors. But not always.

Beware of building a PR strategy on a cult of personality, because that personality — the founder and face of the brand — will inevitably say something they'll regret. Our fractured culture makes the consequences of these misstatements and missteps pretty dire. Even diehard fans may abandon the brand. Eventually the charismatic founder-owner will be yesterday's news and will have to do something even more outrageous to get media attention.

The founder-owner can certainly speak for the brand — but the story she tells should only marginally be about her. It's about why the brand exists.

The snack company LesserEvil is a brand that gets PR right. The founder has just the right mix of charisma and humility — CEO Charles Coristine purchased the company in 2011 and turned it into a clean-ingredient-focused brand. But he knows that the brand's story is bigger than his story. Their grain-free puffed snacks and organic gourmet popcorn appeal to people on the Paleo diet, so the brand has scored coverage and endorsements from dieticians and bloggers who write about the Paleo lifestyle. LesserEvil's WHY — "making our world less evil by creating deeper connections with people, the planet and real, organic food" — drives the media conversation.

## LesserEvil Manifesto

---

Snacking has changed. Once relegated to mindless grazing with limited choices, snacking has become a crucial part of our on-the-go, modern life. Today, life is jammed with choices. Enough that we forget that life is a journey we are all taking together. We crave flavor. We hunger for enlightenment. We need balance. That's why LesserEvil makes snacks. Sinfully tasty snacks made from clean, sustainable ingredients. It's a lot of work, but it's not just food, it's who you are.[a]

---

## What Makes for a Great PR Strategy?

Beloved & Dominant brands adopt a PR strategy that is fully authentic and doesn't read like advertising. Passionate fans of

BFY brands respond to simple storytelling that sounds evangelical because someone — whom they know and trust — is espousing the benefits of a product or brand with authority and expertise.

---

*"What's different now compared to the '80s and '90s is that the consumer has totally changed. Back then, we had a huge job just convincing people that spending a little more for their food was the right thing to do and that they should explore new types of products. Today, consumers, especially younger ones, demand quality and variety. They don't even shop in the center of the store anymore."* — Greg Steltenpohl[4]

---

**Leverages subject matter experts.** Food and consumer journalism are changing; there are fewer traditional print publications and more digital outlets like food and lifestyle blogs. These channels are run by people who are not journalists in the conventional sense — they may not be trained as such, may not employ standard reporting and research, may have a biased point of view — but they are knowledgeable about foods, trends, ingredients, supplements, and related topics. They are passionate about the subject they cover and understand how brands fit into the landscape. Many of these bloggers with big followings wind up landing book deals — so traditional media is paying attention to them, just as their readers are.

**Blends media and audiences.** It's really difficult to get a story into a mass-market print lifestyle magazine (but certainly worth pursuing, if you have a unique enough brand story). Well-regarded food and lifestyle blogs with large and active followings are viable channels, too. Dominant brands also make sure their competitors know what they're doing by leveraging media exposure in trade press, both online and in print.

**Thinks bigger picture.** The BFY space is ripe for context: context surrounding why brands exist and why products are better. Brand marketers and their PR advisors know that placing an article takes more than pitching a product's features and benefits but, rather, pitching a more compelling larger story. For example, LesserEvil earns media coverage from bloggers focused on the vegan life-style, who write about how the product fits into a guilt-free, plant-based diet.

**Doesn't just share news.** In a similar vein, brands that succeed in the PR game don't just issue press releases to announce new products or new retail partners. They share stories: How are consumers using their products in the real world? Who are the farmers who supply ingredients? Why does the brand support community projects? Remember: The objective is to broadcast your ethos, your guiding light, your WHY.

## PR: Who's Doing It Well?

## Chloe's Fruit

Chloe's Fruit founder Chloe Epstein started making a soft-serve ice cream alternative in 2009 by blending fruit, water, and a touch of organic cane sugar. She now operates a flagship store in New York City and sells frozen pops in 10,000 grocery stores across the country.

For such a simple product, the brand has scored outsized pub-licity in traditional media and the blogosphere alike. Forbes and HuffPost picked up its origin story of a female entrepreneur, former lawyer, "fro-yo" addict who became concerned about added sugar and artificial ingredients while pregnant with her first child. Other articles touted Chloe's as a fun treat that makes you feel like you're on vacation, and as a healthy post-workout snack. When the brand landed an opportunity through Chobani Food Incubator for financial and mentoring support, more press coverage followed. Chloe's Fruit was tagged by CNBC as one of seven food companies poised to "take on Big Food."

Note that none of these articles were focused exclusively on the product itself — its taste, flavor combinations, even calorie count. The brand does a great job of what marketing guru Marty Neumeier writes about in his book, "ZAG": Find a parade, and get to the front. Media outlets are embracing the brand's authentic, honest, aspirational story.

## Califia Farms

This Beloved & Dominant brand absolutely fires on all cylinders: compelling story, great product, killer packaging. And its media exposure leverages all of that. It helps that the founder of the company, Greg Steltenpohl, had a raft of experience, both positive and negative, in the BFY beverage market.

Steltenpohl's mantra is, "You can criticize the food industry, or legislate it, or you can just create something different, something better." In 1980, he founded Odwalla, and the fresh organic juice company took off, going public in 1993 before being acquired by The Coca-Cola Co. in 2001 for north of $180 million. But Odwalla went through the wringer in a very public way in 1996, when a fatal outbreak of E. coli was linked to contaminated fruit used in one of its juices. No doubt that experience plays into Califia's very considered media presence.

Steltenpohl crafted a powerful mythology for the alt-dairy brand — a fictional warrior queen named Califia (originally spelled Calafia in the Spanish novel that introduced her legend) who is dubbed "the spirit of California." Like the legendary queen, Califia is committed to shepherding natural resources, a mission that underpins its commitment to a plant-based diet.

Califia's press page is laden with an eye-popping number of links to media articles about the brand. (Seriously: Keep clicking the "Load More" button at the bottom of the page; we'll wait here while you scroll through.) There's a report in a vegan consumer magazine about the brand's new "ubermilk" and its promise to upend the dairy industry (talk about fighting against an ideological enemy), a Forbes piece on Califia's entry into the barista-friendly oat milk niche, and update on Leonardo DiCaprio's investment in the company.

Even articles that aren't about the product itself (like coverage on the packaging design website TheDieline.com) quote Steltenpohl on the brand's mission and quality ingredients. The company's PR machine is built on its consumer education platform. The brand essentially came out of nowhere; now everybody knows them — thanks to a radically disruptive vessel combined with a powerful PR engine that's spread the word well beyond the vegan audience.

## All PR Is Good PR, But That Doesn't Mean It's Smart PR

Ask yourself: Do we have a compelling story? Are we easily gaining earned media? We caution all founders, brand owners, and people looking for a PR agency: Just because you get your brand mentioned in stories doesn't necessarily mean they're the right placements. Quantity does not necessarily equal quality.

Recently we had a new client that was featured in the same issue of a nationally respected health magazine in two different articles. While the PR firm was busy high-fiving over cocktails to celebrate their double placement, we had to gently point out to the client that the first article was about the evils of their category (listing them as least evil) and the other was about which health benefits were absent in their product.

First, know who you are as a brand, what promises you will make, and how you want to show up. Then, know your target audience and how they consume media.

## Your Competitive Audit: PR

1.  Is your PR focused on features and benefits, or are you telling a story that inspires people to recall your brand and want to get involved?

2.  Do you have a laser-focused agenda that says no to opportunities to gain coverage by media that would steer your brand in the wrong direction — or are you happy to just be written about?

3.  Are you easily gaining earned media as a result of your PR efforts?

# Chapter 3

# Advertising: Inviting the Right People Into the Tribe

*figure 3-1: The Brand Ecosystem, Advertising*

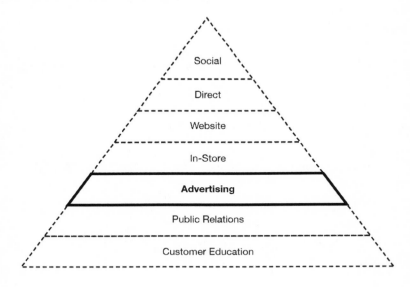

*"Half the money I spend on advertising is wasted; the trouble is I don't know which half."* — John Wanamaker[1]

The internet has upended everything. It's certainly upended advertising.

Before we had computers in our pockets and handbags, before sponsored content flooded our social media channels — before there was such a thing as social media — marketers bought advertising space. Full-page ads, fractional ads, single-column ads, 60-second spots, 30-second spots, billboards, and bus-stop panels.

And they paid advertising agencies, with their brilliant copywriters and art directors and teams of designers, lots of money to fill all those spaces. Pitch meetings, client lunches, photoshoots with well-paid models, custom typefaces, more client lunches.

Advertising is expensive.
And it's losing relevance.

Armed with a great customer education platform anchored by a compelling and ownable brand story (that's the baseline of our Brand Ecosystem pyramid, which we addressed in Chapter 1) and a smart social strategy (which we'll cover in Chapter 7), Beloved & Dominant BFY brands have less expensive channels for spreading the word.

## Consumers Are No Longer Captive

What's more, BFY brands are engaging in conversation with their audience, not just blasting a message via an ad campaign.

Marketers are moving away from "command and control" methodologies — pushing their offering out to a world that had little choice but to receive the message.

## Beloved & Dominant Brands

---

Have a compelling WHY
Know who their tribe is
Talk with — not at — their devotees

---

Think about it: There's really no such thing as a "captive audience" for advertising anymore. Consumers are choosing, in fact paying, to actively avoid advertising. They watch TV and movies ad-free on Netflix, employ technological fixes to block invasive advertising messages online, pay for ad-free apps, and subscribe to receive adless digital content. We modern humans have rewired our brains to ignore invasive communications like banner ads and popups. Consumers, not marketers, are fully in control of the ads they see, or don't.

---

*"Mobile applications have fundamentally changed the ad industry. People are especially intolerant of interruptions on their mobile devices because they are so personal, and the age-old precept of reach and frequency is becoming outdated. Additionally, advertisers can pinpoint specific people they want to reach on any device rather than relying on editorial environments to attract them. On one hand, these factors are creating more efficient advertising mechanisms; on the other, the power is shifting to consumers who are demanding more relevant and entertaining experiences in exchange for their attention."* — Mitchell Reichgut[1]

---

That said, brands need ways to provoke people to think about their products. They need to communicate how they are meaningfully different in a way that's impossible to ignore. Advertising excels when it's eye-catching, disruptive, declarative. It's about stopping consumers in their tracks and demanding attention. It's repetition. But it really is more of an art than a science.

---

Who's in your tribe and how will they recognize your call?

---

Beloved & Dominant brands leverage the intrusive, one-way nature of advertising and use it as a sort of "Bat-Signal" that projects into the world and calls their tribe to gather.

## Advertising as a Call to Your Tribe

If PR is how you get respected third parties talking about you, then advertising is how you talk about yourself to the marketplace.

Advertising has always been about building awareness, and that's still true. But without a basis in the brand's WHY, it's just shouting into the wind. (That's the useless expense of advertising dollars that our friend Mr. Wanamaker was concerned about at the beginning of the chapter.)

So many brands ride a roller coaster of ineffective advertising. Given enough investment in quote-unquote award-winning creative and blitzkrieg multichannel placement, advertising can goose sales temporarily. And when the campaign ends, sales slow back down. People may try the product, intrigued by that billboard they saw on the drive home. When the billboard goes away, so does consumer awareness.

When advertising is connected back to the brand's WHY and prompts engagement with the brand in a deeper way, the resulting sales lift lasts beyond the duration of a campaign.

# For Beloved & Dominant Brands, Advertising Is ...

**A badge or password.** Advertising can, through repetition, indelibly associate a brand with a graphic mark that fans can wear or a tagline that they can repeat to show they're in the tribe. ("Dilly dilly," anyone?) The Nike swoosh is a brilliant tribal totem: When you run into other people wearing Nike gear, you see the badge and you have that social proof that you're in the right tribe with other people you identify with.

**A visual 'snack.'** Digital channels, where everyone is scrolling through social feeds and clicking away pop-up ads, have accelerated the messaging pace. Advertising has to be super quick to catch the eye and to consume. Copy has to be easily digested in just one mental bite; video has to function as a 6-second Instagram story. The days when advertisers could play clever and ask their audiences to read, let alone think are long gone.

**A prompt to action.** Advertising doesn't have to tell the full story of the brand. Its role is to inspire those who know just enough about the brand to be curious, and those who think they may be ready to join the converted. Advertising should prompt those eager would-bes to seek out the brand's consumer education platform to learn more. That's where the conversion happens.

And advertising should remind long-term fans why the brand exists, keeping them engaged. Advertising reassures them that everything else they've seen from and about the brand is true. They see the ad and say, "Yep, that's it. That's me. I'm in."

**An extended hand.** Categories within the BFY space tend to have these "insider baseball" conversations happening; they talk amongst themselves using jargon and cleverness. This in-the-know approach is an easy strategy for marketers within that category — you just have to deploy a few keywords that everyone already knows — but it's too opaque for consumers who don't already know the brand or category. With this strategy, there's no opportunity for brands to grow or new audiences to stem from the campaign. Instead, advertising should extend a welcoming hand to consumers who may be circling just outside the group awaiting an invitation to join.

**A velvet rope.** Once you identify who's in your tribe, you have permission to keep the nonbelievers out. Advertising can function like a bouncer outside a fashionable club who casts a discerning eye and waves the right kind of guest into the party. This may feel counterintuitive at first — why would a brand want to turn people away? But it's the best way to generate real growth because it invites like-minded humans to come to you.

Remember, Beloved & Dominant brands are those whose unique story and passionate audience combine to make it virtually competition-proof. Play to the masses, lower your threshold, and you'll almost certainly be reduced to One of Many.

This is where advertising gets more into the art than the science. Successful advertising that speaks to your tribe comes down to tone and voice. You must make sure your tribe can recognize your unique call. This is what a good friend of ours calls "the dog whistle." Only those you've identified as members of your tribe will hear your brand's silent call, and leave all others unable to hear it and, therefore, unable to opt in to your brand.

*"Digital advertising will become less interruptive and more relevant. Currently, anyone who can afford to pay about $12 per month can avoid ads on platforms like Amazon, YouTube, Netflix, etc. The onus will increasingly be on advertisers to provide value in exchange for people's attention."* —Mitchell Reichgut[2]

## Is Your Advertising Memorable?

There's no better way to throw good advertising dollars after bad than to create a campaign that is neither ownable nor memorable. (If only so many Super Bowl advertisers weren't guilty of this.) And there's an incredibly easy way to determine if a brand's campaign is generic and forgettable: Simply swap in a competitor's logo to see if the ads are interchangeable.

A communication audit will reveal if your brand is guilty of the sin of nondescript advertising, and it's an essential part of any competitive audit. Gather all your brand materials in a row: printouts of your homepage, your digital and print ad campaigns, packaging, all of it. Do the same with two or three key competitors. What do you see? Now literally cut and paste the brands' logos over each other. Do they still all look and feel alike, or is it obvious that one brand has a distinct and ownable communication strategy that can't be substituted for another in consumers' eyes?

## Advertising: Who's Doing it Well?

## Halo Top

Building on a great origin story that generated a ton of consumer buzz, Halo Top managed to blow expectations out of the water for seven years without any substantial advertising.

Word of mouth has propelled Halo Top's loyal following. Sales in 2016 jumped about 2,500% from 2015.[a]

The BFY ice cream brand, which launched in 2012, leveraged PR and social channels to gather a cult following, with online outlets eagerly reporting on new flavors and bloggers touting the "secret menu" at Halo Top scoop shops. They rock packaging, too, with the number of calories per pint — not per serving, mind you; per pint — right on the front of the carton.

The brand's first national TV campaign debuted in 2019, the work of 72andSunny New York. The spots are darkly funny, in keeping with the brand's overall voice, and aimed squarely at their target audience: adults. Backed by a super catchy jingle at the end, a narrator adds the tagline, "Ice cream for adults, 'cause adults need a lot of ice cream."

It hits on two key strategies we've mentioned: Calling out to the tribe of Halo Top devotees in a voice they recognize as their own, and catching the attention of people intrigued enough about the brand to learn more about it … and then to try.

## Bubly

PepsiCo was fairly late to the flavored seltzer water game, but the category was ripe for big-brand dominance thanks to the consumer buzz sparked by early-in brands like LaCroix. The category is mature enough by now that brands don't have to work hard to educate customers on the features and benefits of naturally flavored fizzy water. So Pepsi built a Super Bowl ad solely aimed at driving awareness with a smart play on the brand name. Featuring Michael Bublé to attract attention placed the brand perfectly into cultural context. The campaign is advertising at its best; think it doesn't work? My kids (and many of their grade school and middle school friends) cross out the logo on the can to make it read Bublé. This is profoundly intelligent cultivation of a future audience that will not be interested in LaCroix. It's not as though Michael Bublé was exactly endorsing Bubly water … he played a role in a 30-second commercial spoof.

## Essentia

Essentia is a water brand that leverages celebrity in a different way. The brand's ethos speaks to hardworking people who need smart hydration, no matter what they're doing. Its core WHY boils down to this: "You know that thing you're going to do? You need to bring your whole soul and mind and body to it. Otherwise, someone else will do it better than you will."

Following a repositioning away from an audience of yoga practitioners to one of dedicated do-ers from all walks of life, Essentia's marketing team cultivated a social media following among overachievers they called Essentia Nation. The message was all about powering an activity — with no reference to the science behind the water (it's ionized and alkalized for better hydration). As a result, the brand realized double the growth of other brands in the "power water" category.

In 2019, the brand tapped four influencers for a national ad campaign, some of them known (quarterback Patrick Mahomes) and some not (award-winning young chef Julian Rodarte). The campaign is taglined, "Someone is going to …" and the implication is that YOU, the true believer, can achieve anything with the right hydration. These are endorsement spots, yes, but tightly knitted together with the brand's WHY.

## Nike

A BFY lifestyle and apparel brand, Nike consistently kills it with advertising. The brand is known for iconic advertising across all channels, but its crown jewel was the late-2018 campaign featuring controversial quarterback Colin Kaepernick. Talk about representing the brand's WHY: Kaepernick, shunned by NFL teams for his kneeling stance during pregame national anthem ceremonies, appeared with the tagline, "Believe in something. Even it if means sacrificing everything." In the face of social media outcry and boycott calls, Nike's sales jumped 10% immediately following the campaign debut, and the company's stock rose in an overall soft Wall Street market on news of strong quarterly earnings.

The campaign spoke to Nike's tribe, saying: "There are no excuses. If you try hard enough and work your butt off, you will be victorious in spite of any obstacle—racism, poverty, lack of opportunity, sexism, whatever it may be. Now go!"

## Advertising, If You Don't Have an Advertising Budget

We'll reiterate: Advertising is expensive. And for that reason, it's the single platform in the Brand Ecosystem that we will advise clients to pare back or eliminate from their strategies.

The paradox of advertising is that it has to be disruptive, and yet consumers are irritated by disruption, especially in the digital space. So before you embark on an ad campaign, be sure you're well-armed with data that confirms that your tribe is so into your message that they won't mind the interruption.

Know who your "people" are. Are they metropolitan residents? If so, an out-of-home campaign may work better than print.

Use microtargeting to deploy the campaign in phases by market segmentation, whether that's geographic or demographic. Run a focused campaign, measure results, iterate, then move to the next segment. Bottom line: Do your research to understand where your audience consumes information, then meet them there.

Top brands with limited ad budgets can see meaningful results if they pivot their ad spend and messaging from the consumer audience to the B2B audience. Especially in the early stage of a brand or product launch, the best channel for advertising aims at retailers and distributors; think trade shows and industry publications, both online and off. Get in front of the people who stand between you and your consumer. Make the right retail partners aware of you, and you'll pave a smoother path to shelf placement and promotional opportunity.

One final tactical note on advertising: To make sure your ads get front of the right people through the right channels at the right times, you need a terrific media buying partner. This person or agency team will show you the data on how your tribe lives, works, and connects.

## When Others Talk About You, You Don't Have to Talk About Yourself

Beloved & Dominant brands with the "cultiest" ideas don't need conventional advertising; between in-store, web, social, and PR, they should have the tools they need to be Robin Hood — stealing business from competing brands.

Advertising is the plank of the Brand Ecosystem pyramid that can drop out if you are an early stage brand and have limited relationships. Instead of investing in marketing funds in advertising, triple-down on your WHY, your customer education, and your PR and make sure that's rock-solid, then build on top of it. Develop your story and get it out there through third-party endorsement and consumer buzz.

If you don't know your WHY, it doesn't matter where you advertise.

## Your Competitive Audit: Advertising

1.  Is your creative a category disruptor?

2.  Could you replace your logo in your ad layouts with that of a competitor and have an ad that works just as well for them as it does for you?

3.  Does your ad clearly express who you are, why you exist, and how you benefit your loyalists?

4.  Are you using the "Pray 'n' Spray" approach to placement — throwing a bunch of messages out on all the channels and hoping for the best? Or are you running highly targeted, research-driven placement based upon analysis of your current customers and your ideal customers-to-be?

5.  What is your ad program's call to action? Are you inspiring your audience to learn more?

# Chapter 4

# In-Store: Whispering in the Shopper's Ear

*figure 4-1: The Brand Ecosystem: In-Store*

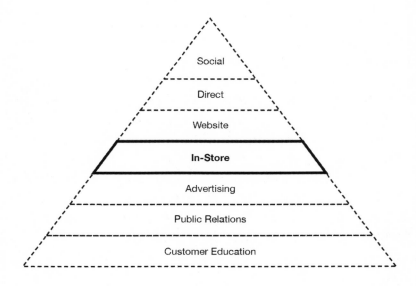

You've begun educating the consumer about your brand's points of differentiation, and you've spread the word through unpaid media exposure and paid promotion.

The in-store experience is when consumers are truly faced with the choice: your brand or another one?

In-store plays an outsized role in the Brand Ecosystem pyramid, because it may be the first time the consumer encounters your brand at all. She may not have heard about you, may have overlooked your website and the information you share there, may not have seen any advertising.

In fact, she may see you on display for the first time and be intrigued enough to whip out her mobile phone right there in the middle of the aisle to look you up online and learn more about your brand promise and your product. (This is why mobile-friendly website design is essential.)

According to a 2015 Google/Ipsos survey, Consumers in the Micro-Moment, 82% of smartphone users say they consult their phones on purchases they're about to make in a store. And if you've done a good job of customer education, your website will seal the deal from a brand perspective right there in the store when she takes out her phone. Beloved & Dominant brands create a seamless experience for the consumer that points from the package to the website and back again.

But you have to catch her eye first.

And that's the science of packaging design. (Though, as we'll see in a moment, success at retail is about far more than having a sexy package.)

## The Science of Retail Packaging

It truly is a science: Packaging is not just about looking cool; it's about being the right kind of visible, with the right mix of points of parity and points of difference. Your package is often your first or only salesperson, so it has to work hard: to attract, to inform, to entice, to convince.

And it has to do all that in the chaos of the retail environment and the thumbnail view of competing products on Amazon.

As you conduct your competitive audit, look at your brand's category in the context of the retail reality, in real time, while real shoppers are browsing your competitive set without the aid of a sales team or a brand activation team or a rep giving out samples. Go to your biggest retail outlet at their busiest time of the week and just watch. What do you see?

*figure 4-2: The 30–10–3 Rule of Retail Packaging*

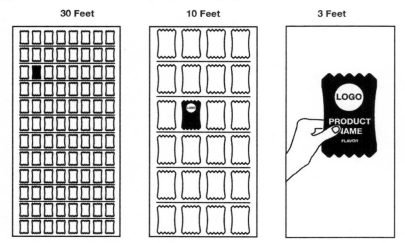

## The 30–10–3 Rule of Retail Packaging

Our basic guideline to evaluate the strength of a brand's in-store presentation is called the 30–10–3 Rule. Here's how it works:

From 30 feet away, your packaging should help identify the category.

From 10 feet away, your consumers should be able to read your brand's trade dress or core identity (and ideally your logo) in order to navigate to it.

From 3 feet away, your brand story, features, benefits, and purpose should be so clear and compelling that consumers pick up your package and allow it to whisper in their ear. After all, once your product is in the shopper's hand, she's more likely to buy.

So, let's break this rule down into its component parts.

# 1. Category Navigation

Here's the simplest way to understand category navigation: Imagine looking for milk in the grocery store. The vessels, varieties, and design language all work together to instantly telegraph milk.

Now let's think about how this might work at REI or Dick's Sporting Goods. Body Glide is a great example of this. The brand used to disappear on the shelf; it looked like every other product within the category. The marketing team reinvented the brand's look such that now they are the category navigator for athletic anti-chafe balm at 30 feet. You can drive straight to it. The brand's color system and identity makes its packaging the de facto category signifier. And this communication happens within seconds, without the consumer even realizing it.

## 2. Brand Blocking

When your product lives on a shelf you don't control in an environment you don't control, brand blocking is crucial. Essentially, this is where a consumer can easily identify your product and all your offerings within that line. Color and identity come into play here. This works even if you only get three facings. If you have a good visual identity system, you'll stand out. No matter how many facings you secure from your retail partners, your packaging will make or break your shelf presence. If the packaging recedes and your competitors, stand out, you could entirely own the shelf and still lose traction. Competing brands with stronger packaging, better brand blocking, and more legible identities stand out and disrupt the shelf more effectively. A whole shelf of "meh" packaging loses to a single facing of a killer package. Every time.

A whole shelf of "meh" packaging loses to a single facing of a killer package.

## 3. Design Aesthetics

When we talk about design aesthetics, we talk about making your brand look like it belongs in the life of today's shopper. It cannot look frumpy, old, or outdated. You don't want to create the impression that your product's been sitting on the shelf since the 1980s.

Yet there's a balancing act, between similar and standout. It's important to match the contemporary visual lexicon of your product category — and at the same time to step to the forefront of that. That's how brands become disruptive at shelf.

Consider in advance what makes the most sense for your brand on the "Different and Similiar" axis.

*figure 4-3* **Standout and Similar**

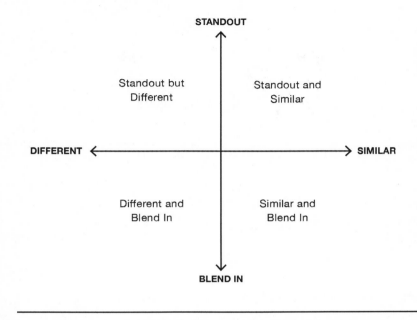

We've adapted branding expert Marty Neumeier's Good/Different Axis to steer you toward the ideal balance between Similar and Standout.[a]

If you can't disrupt, your brand will likely compete on price. And nobody wins on price, except Walmart.

## Packaging That Whispers in Your Ear

As we've discussed, sometimes the shelf is the only touchpoint the consumer has with your brand. You need to make sure your brand can show up in a meaningful way to prompt your potential consumer to give you permission to whisper in her ear.

We use the Flip Test to gauge how captivating a package is. You can conduct your own Flip Test the next time you find yourself waiting in line at Starbucks. Take notice the carefully curated offering of innovative snacks. Then, notice how intimate their packaging feels. Pay attention as you instinctively flip the package over in order to engage in its ingredients, nutrition content, brand promise, and narrative.

## Retail Domination Takes More Than Packaging

Retail managers will tell you that they're facing an apocalypse. And they're only partly exaggerating. The traditional middle-class buyer is getting squeezed. Household and consumer goods costs almost across the board are more expensive in today's dollars than in their parents' prime, and wages haven't kept up.

At the same time, consumers have endless choices. The combination of less liquidity in household income plus more choice means that consumers are less brand-loyal today than ever. They're price sensitive, so margins are thinner than ever. And they're incredibly time pressed, so they choose products more quickly than ever.

While this economic shift is real, retailers themselves have a hand in creating this apocalypse. That's because they haven't kept up with the new wave of consumers and their unique wants and needs.

Today's core consumer is the Xennial — she's part of a micro-generation between Gen X and millennials. She exhibits characteristics of both: tech savvy, yet wary of tech's role in our lives, cynical yet optimistic, skeptical of brands yet using them to build her own identity.

# Chapter 4: In-Store: Whispering in the Shopper's Ear

At my agency, we call her the Gatekeeper Mom.

*figure 4-4: Gatekeeper Mom*

She's making choices and building an identity for herself out of the brands she chooses. She's willing to spend more on brands that align with her vision of herself, and she'll spend less on other things.

And she's a bit of a contradiction. She may favor BFY beauty, food, and beverage brands, but she's no die-hard granola-eating hippie like her parents were — she buys organic kale and then drives home in her gas-guzzling SUV. Even though she shops online, she wants her in-store experience to be special.

Retail managers — and the brands they place on shelves — had better recognize the new customer they're competing for.

## Make Retailers Your Allies

Thanks to the so-called Retail Apocalypse, the category manager within the retail company is under immense pressure to get his category to perform well and make as much margin through velocity as possible. And the people he reports to — the retailer's executive team — are merciless and swift in making changes should he be less than successful.

But know that most of these managers are passionate about the category, too. They want to co-author your success story. They can be key collaborators in your brand strategy process. And when you turn their input into products, they'll be the first to place an order. Relationships with these retail managers are essential, and nurturing them requires that your reps are regularly meeting with them in person.

## 5 Ways to Increase Velocity at Key Retailers

1. Relationship building
2. Secondary displays
3. Driving trial through passive or active sampling
4. Placement/brand blocking
5. Effective pricing strategy

## In-Store: Who's Doing it Well?

## REI

If you're looking for the paradigm of the in-store experience, consider REI. Yes, this outdoor outfitter has complete control over its retail experience, something not available to all BFY brands. Don't let that keep you from learning from this Beloved & Dominant brand.

# Chapter 4: In-Store: Whispering in the Shopper's Ear

I asked REI's Chief Customer Officer Ben Steele why going to an REI such a mecca-like experience for fans of the brand. I wanted to know what customers experience in the store that they don't get from other touchpoints with the brand. "Modern brands = relationships," he told me.

*"The goal of any misson-driven, purpose-led, or passion brand — whatever you want to call it — should be relationships.*

*Brands should be all about creating and building mutual value. As a member or customer of REI, I feel like a better version of myself when I am participating in my membership at any level. The REI store is organized around the relationship the brand has with the members; the people who shop and the people who work share the same values,"* Ben said.

Ben talks about the interconnectedness of the brand and its audience — which can apply even to brands that don't control their retail space.

*"When I was in college, my friends and I would drive to the flagship store in Seattle and spend hours dreaming about the adventures we had back home and would have in the future,"* he recalled. *"The store is mecca-like because it's a connected experience; you automatically connect with your history and your dream of adventuring in the outdoors at whatever level is deep and personal for you. And you have permission to deepen your relationship with the brand by sharing stories, getting the right gear, and discovering new places to explore. All of this passion is why our organization exists."*

# DRY Soda

In 2010, DRY Soda captured industry attention thanks to its award-winning packaging. It looked great on the shelf. The brand had basically invented the craft soda category. And then competitors flooded the soda aisle and DRY was lost in the shuffle. The brand was on the ropes; the sales team resorted to discounts and promotions in order to stay in business. Product only moved when it was on deal 10 for $10, when it wasn't on sale, it didn't move.

The underlying problem was that retail managers didn't know where to shelve the product. DRY's flavor profile is more culinary and subtler than craft orange soda and rootbeer, the other drivers in the category. So consumers who bought DRY Soda expecting that big soda taste were disappointed.

DRY repositioned its flagship product line as DRY Sparkling, an unexpectedly crisp sparkling beverage, more akin to naturally flavored fizzy water, a more interesting version of LaCroix and a lighter option than San Pellegrino sodas. Then the company's sales team pled their case with retailers about where the brand should be placed, how it should be positioned, and how it should be priced. Retail category managers were skeptical. But when DRY made a pitch to a major retailer and secured the primary position in the flavored water. And in the first three years, DRY saw 20x growth in sales.

Talking to retail managers was the key.

How well do your brand leaders understand what the retail buyer needs and how to speak about the category to help them reach their goals? Winning the retail game means teaming up with the retail category buyer to help him curate the category, not just slot in all the cheapest products. Category managers need brand owners to have a strong point of view about how the brand and its ethos fit within the retail ecosystem.

---

How well do your brand leaders understand what the retail buyer needs and how to speak about the category to help them reach their goals?

---

When you can build strong relationships with retail buyers, incredible things happen. Retailers think you're their idea because they hear their voice in the solution you come up with. They feel a sense of co-authoring; their category definition is tighter and better formed; and they feel more authoritative and on trend. This level of partnership insulates you from other challenges because retailers will go out of their way to help you win; if your volume drops or if you have a sales promotion issue, they'll be able to support you.

Rocking your in-store presence isn't just about packaging or point-of-purchase. It's about building relationships with someone who can make or break your business.

## One Caveat About Retail Relationships

As you're pursuing deeper partnerships with retail managers, don't depend overly much on their input. It can become a 900-pound gorilla.

One of our clients risked relying way too heavily on feedback from Whole Foods. The retailer was pushing the brand to go organic and sustainable, but there was no way to economically source the volume of organic ingredients needed to make the product. The math didn't work.

We helped reframe the conversation in a way that addressed the Whole Foods' buyer's concern. Sourcing organic ingredients would have put the company out of business; they would have had to price the product at double the cost of competing products. It was unsustainable. And that's where we guided the conversation, by teaching the Whole Foods buyers that sustainability isn't just environmental; it's economic. It also means helping small businesses and medium-sized businesses thrive. Sometimes, you'll have to lead the category manager to the decision that's right for both you and the retailer. It's a matter of mutually assured success instead of mutually assured destruction.

## Your Competitive Audit: In-Store

1. Can you identify the category conventions shoppers need from products like yours?

2. Does your in-store presence stop traffic? Is your brand and packaging disruptive on the shelf?

3. How successfully does your packaging communicate your products points of parity and points of difference?

4. Do you know if you are working with the category manager or the retail buyer? Do you know the difference?

5. Have you researched your category deeply enough to become a spokesperson for it? If so, what would you say?

6. Does your in-store expression follow the 30–10—3– Rule?

7. How can you better engage your retail partners to optimize your in-store experience?

# Chapter 5

# Website: Creating the Hub of Your Brand's Storytelling Universe

*figure 5-1: The Brand Ecosystem: Website*

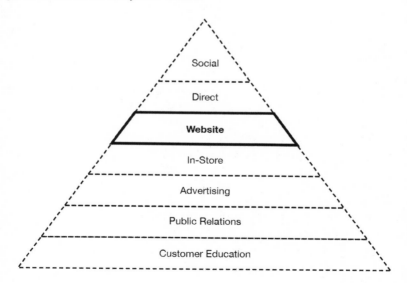

When a shopper is standing in the grocery aisle and wants to learn more about your brand of BFY puffed snacks, where does he go? When a fan of your brand wants to tell her friends how healthy your gluten-free granola bars are, where can she find ingredients and nutrition facts? When a consumer wants to purchase a case of your vitamin-enhanced water, where can he do that?

A BFY brand's website is the hub for all activity — information, inspiration, commerce. It's the sun around which the marketing universe orbits.

## The Customer Journey Revolves Around the Website

Let's take another look at a Customer Journey Map, which we explored in Chapter 1. While it's commonly used in B2B marketing to describe how buyers evaluate and choose products and services, it also charts how consumers decide how and what to purchase in their everyday lives, from big-ticket items like automobiles to routine things like BFY snacks and haircare products.

Every step of the customer journey touches a brand's website. Every one. It's where the customer turns to:

- Learn more about the product
- Research ingredients and nutritional claims
- Compare it to other brands she's considering, and decide if it's worth the price
- Purchase online (and we'll get more in-depth on this in a moment) and re-order
- Stay connected with the brand's latest news
- Gather information she'll use to convince her friends how great the product is

The digital world and the physical world come together on your brand's website. So it needs to be deep, robust, and chock-full of information; a place where people feel they can spend time learning about your brand. You want your customer to be able to come to your site and dig deep into who you are, why you exist, and how they can get involved. Use your website to move visitors from merely buying products to a place where they can connect to everything your brand stands for beyond the transaction.

## A Brand's Website Fuels Spending

A few fun facts:

- Nearly half (47%) of mobile shoppers are also doing so on desktop devices
- Before making big purchases, approximately 81% of shoppers default to online research
- Google research shows that:

  ◊ 43% of consumers who shop the consumer packaged goods (CPG) category said they used search in their most recent shopping journey to become inspired, browse, or research
  ◊ Spending 50% more than those who didn't use search
  ◊ Shoppers who visit brands' websites or mobile apps to browse or research before or during their journey report spending 108% more than people who don't

In other words, consumers go online to research before they buy, and they spend more when they've done that research — and furthermore, when they land on YOUR website, they'll more than double their total purchase of your brand.

## Let the Consumer Control Their Web Experience

Because the consumer has navigated by her own actions to your website, she and the brand are on equal footing. You both have permission to interact: you to share information and she to control the pace at which she moves through it. The website should allow her to discover your brand at her own pace, free of distraction. If she's on your website, in your world, you have permission to slow down. How slow and how much is contextual to your brand, how complicated your sell is, and how transformative it is to your customer.

By contrast, other channels through which you might communicate with her move at high speed and are full of noise: the store environment, the social media space, the YouTube channel. It's like being in a library as opposed to being in an airport. Envision your product in Hudson News at JFK, but your website is the top floor of the library in your city — a place for leisurely discovery.

Give the consumer all the information she might need in a way that's easy to find, and then get out of her way. Let her fall in love with your brand on her own terms.

## A Website is NOT

The web is very meta; it's full of information about the web. How to build a website, how to design a great user experience, how to track traffic, and so on. You already have a website, certainly, so advice on how to create one isn't especially helpful.

It's more instructive to explore all the things that a website should NOT be.

# 1. A Website Is Not a Brochure

It is not a static, finished piece that a reader might page through start to finish. A website should be alive and constantly changing so that people — and Google, which elevates search results based on dynamic content — have a reason to come back to it. Know that users will come to your site by many different paths: via a link they spotted on Facebook, via dialing up your mobile version on his phone, via searching for an ingredient. And they'll land on your site in different places, not necessarily the homepage.

So allow them to "choose their own adventure." No matter where a visitor enters, he can easily navigate to information that is relevant to him, all while being surprised and delighted along the way.

Your brand lives in a communication ecosystem, and the website is just one component thereof. Which means you need to think about the kind of content you produce, how it's getting out into the world, where people are likely to find it, and how they might come to the site. Once you have customers on the site, you must figure out how to guide them to take action.

# 2. A Website is Not Gallery of Product

If a shopper wants to see a page full of product, he'll navigate to Amazon. If he's come to your site, he's looking for information. And that's especially important in the BFY food, supplement, and skincare space, where products tend to feature functional or uncommon ingredients that consumers need an introduction to. If your product is a complex sell, your website is the holding tank for all that essential information.

Good packaging can be the bridge out to a customer education platform — which is what your website should be — because consumers looking for deeper information on product claims can find more details about the product's features and benefits. The FDA regulates what food and beverage brands can declare on their packaging. But the website can talk about your product claims in long-form content using language that appeals to consumers emotions.

## 3. A Website Is Not a Mask

You'll recall the scene in "The Wizard of Oz," where the wizard, a self-proclaimed "humbug" stands at a console where he controls the fearsome visage projected in the next room. "Pay no attention to the man behind the curtain," the face of Oz booms menacingly.

Your website is not a curtain. It shouldn't hide truth.

Anything is findable on the web, so every false claim you make is easily debunked, every negative review you receive is easily surfaced. In today's experience economy, consumers are continually having to choose between real and fake. They'll judge you on authenticity and truthfulness.

If your website communicates in a tone and vocabulary that rings false to your brand ethos, if your origin story doesn't have a trail of truth running all the way through it, if you've willingly concealed less-than-savory aspects of how you do business, visitors will know. If you claim to be a healthy brand and your ingredient list contains artificial fillers, consumers will smell a fake. If you tell your story in an inauthentic way, everyone's BS meter will sound an alarm.

## 4. A Website Is Not a Desktop-Only Experience

All those shoppers who report using online search to guide their purchasing decisions ... those shoppers who spend more as a result of their search? Where do you think they're doing that research? At their desks at home?

Recall this data point from Chapter 4:

---

82% of smartphone users say they consult their phones on purchases they're about to make in a store[a]

---

Most web platforms today automatically render a mobile version of a website, so it's not a matter of simply having a mobile-friendly brand website. Rather, the site should be optimized for mobile. Anticipate what those shoppers who consult their phones in the moment of purchase will need from you, and deliver that information first and foremost.

## 5. A Website Is Not a Hard Sales Pitch

You've intrigued the consumer enough to get her to spend time on your website. Respect that time by not bombarding her with promo codes and discount offers. Instead, focus on your brand's WHY — your reasons for being and behaving in the world. What are you here for beyond selling product and making money?

Remember, Beloved & Dominant brands rise above the many competitors in their space because they exist to solve a problem, right a wrong, serve a purpose. This brand ethos wins converts willing to pay a premium for branded products that align with their own worldview.

---

*"Mutual value and relationship and respect is what consumers are looking for. They can buy something from a lot of outlets. But the value they place on their relationship with a brand and its ability to make them a better version of themselves is what people crave more than the 20% off. Even though that 20% off is also important, it's not the brand. If a brand is more than a discount, if it becomes a place the consumer goes to learn, to be inspired, to be challenged about their life and their passions, then that brand is irreplaceable in that customer's everyday life."* — Ben Steele, REI Chief Customer Officer[1]

---

# Make It Easy to Buy Online

That said ... don't stand in the way of the customer who's ready to make a purchase RIGHT NOW. While you're not leading with the sale, you're not closing the door on it either. Don't make a visitor read through four pages of information in order to give you her money; mix the education and reassurance in, but keep the shopping channel available at all times.

The website's goal is to deliver information that inspires the consumer to become a stark raving fan. They've chosen to engage with your brand, so there's an implicit understanding that you'll ask them to buy. If you get someone interested in your product and he could be one click away from putting it in his shopping cart, why would you stop that natural progression and risk the best possible conversion? The sale might happen through your ecommerce platform, but it doesn't have to; link to Amazon or whatever online selling channels you employ, or make it easy for the visitor to find a "Where to Buy" page. BFY marketers have the habit of thinking it's wrong to focus on the conversion, but that's untrue on your website, because consumers have come to you.

## Your Website's Primary Mission: Telling Your Story

Storytelling is the new marketing. The very position of a Beloved & Dominant brand hinges on its relationship with its audience, and there's no more powerful way to forge a deep connection than through story. Beloved & Dominant companies recognize storytelling as a core business competency essential to growth.

---

*"People are attracted to stories because we're social creatures and we relate to other people."* — Keith Quesenberry[2]

---

There is no better way to convey the essence of your brand— **your promise and the way you keep it**—than through storytelling.

Storytelling is especially potent for BFY brands because story matters in this context. Food connects people. Stories connect people. Where and when do we share stories with one another? Over dinner or drinks. Humans have done this for millennia. Story is elemental to who we are.

Great brand stories may not change the world, but they will let your target market understand why your brand is worth their time and money.

*"If you want to know me, then you must know my story, for my story defines who I am."* — Dan McAdams[3]

The ideal channel for sharing your story — of your brand and your products — is your website. That's because you shape the message and control its presentation. A narrative, editorial-style approach to website content surrounds the brand with context, emotion, meaning.

Great storytelling can:

- Make a strong case for buying your products over others, and for buying your products regardless of price
- Give customers a sense of shared ownership in the brand
- Arm your loyalists with talking points they can use when they evangelize on your behalf
- Help people identify as part of the tribe, because they see themselves in your story

*"Consumers are oversaturated with information. As a business, it's all too easy to blend into the noise. A business may genuinely have a better product or service than a competitor, but at the end of the day, decision-making is much more emotional than it is logical. The ability to tell a good story is essential and can make or break how well a business differentiates itself in the market as well as makes a profit."*

No matter the medium, a compelling story follows a well-established narrative structure. It unfolds at an intentional pace. There's a lead character. A challenge. Some tension or drama. Perseverance and accomplishment. Growth and success.

# The 12 Brand Archetypes and Narrative Styles

Pioneering Swiss psychologist Carl Jung suggested that human personalities follow one of 12 archetypes, which have become part of the psychology canon. Marketers subsequently adapted these personality types to create a set of 12 archetypes to describe a brand's persona and ethos. This concept provides a helpful tool for imagining how the brand communicates with its audience and, by extension, the type of audience it attracts. And the brand's narrative approach logically flows from the archetype.

| | |
|---|---|
| **The Everyman/ Woman** | I'm just like you, and I'm sharing the products that I love with you |
| **The Hero** | I've overcome my struggle and can help you with yours |
| **The Innocent** | I want you to be happy |
| **The Outlaw** | I'm bucking the system and I want you, as a fellow rebel, to join me |
| **The Explorer** | I want to help you get out of your rut, find a new path, live your best life |
| **The Artist** | I've made the perfect product that's just right for you |
| **The Ruler** | I've curated this special product line just for those highly selective people who are in the know |
| **The Magician** | I can help make all your dreams come true |
| **The Lover** | I want you to treat yourself, enjoy the pleasures in life |
| **The Caregiver** | I'm here with products that will take care of you and make you feel healthy and well |
| **The Jester** | I'm all about having fun, and you'll enjoy yourself when you use my products |
| **The Sage** | I can guide you through the noise and chaos to find something that works just for you |

# BELOVED & DOMINANT BRANDS

There are lots of different ways to craft a brand story. Beloved & Dominant brands tell stories that stand out from their competitors, in a voice and persona that's distinct and ownable, in ways that are fresh and unexpected.

Let's look at some food brands with killer stories:

*Just like our products, we're different. We like to zig when others zag. We don't see obstacles. We work hard, play fair and laugh a lot. We're bold. We take pride in helping people eat healthier. We're a 3rd generation female-owned family business operating in a male-dominated industry.* — Frieda's[b]

*Our mantra around food is that we would not put anything in our foods that we wouldn't feed our own children; If you know my family, you know we take eating pretty seriously. In addition to my family's commitment to eating organic, we stay away from processed foods, refined sugars and acidic foods. We believe in a whole food, plant-based diet that is high in alkalinity.* — Lesser Evil[c]

*As a food-allergy sufferer, Hilary knew first-hand how difficult it could be to find healthy, convenient foods, free from common food allergens and artificial ingredients. She wanted to create a great-tasting, go-to product for all kinds of eaters.* — Hilary's Eat Well[d]

*When I became pregnant with my first child, I started paying more attention to the quality of the foods I was eating. I started experimenting with fruit in juicers, blenders, cuisinarts—you name it! Following countless recipes, tons of frozen bananas and lots of patience, Chloe's Fruit was born using just fruit, water, and a touch of cane sugar.* — Chloe's Fruit[e]

Consumers can see themselves in these brand stories: women fighting for a fair shake, those struggling with food allergies or dietary restrictions, health-minded parents who want to do the right thing for their kids.

## Websites: Who's Doing it Well?

# REI

REI.com is the center of the Beloved & Dominant outdoor out-fitter's marketing universe — even though it leans heavily on its retail spaces to create community with fans. It all sings from the same songbook: "The REI brand is in every single touchpoint, and every single touchpoint reflects the brand," Ben Steele, REI's Chief Customer Officer, told me.

When I asked Ben about how the brand balances the sales pro-cess online, he stressed the importance of sharing content that truly reflects the site visitor's interests. *"Our theory is, 'Let us meet you where you are.' If you just Googled 'new boots,' we had better show you new boots. And if you want to learn too, we will make that available to you, but if you come in seeking product, the product needs to come first. However, if you come in after watching a 6-minute video we shared on YouTube about the principles of healing your spirit in the outdoors, then we know you want a lot more than boots and we will make that available to you."*

He continued, *"At REI, we are doing a good job of telling sto-ries. I am incredibly proud of the work we do and how we show up. REI doesn't feel like there is a Wizard of Oz behind a curtain somewhere. It feels authentic because it is authentic."*

For example, he told me, the marketing team pays close attention to the brand's visual representation, including lifestyle and product photography. *"We ask ourselves on every shoot, 'Are the people in the photo members? Do they represent the diversity and makeup of our real membership?"*

For REI, brand and customer experience are one and the same, no matter the channel.

## SoulCycle

A true BFY brand, SoulCycle has come up with a powerful story to compel people to pay close to the price equivalent of a monthly membership at your typical gym — for one 45-minute class. While this brand does offer a high-end fitness experience, with a focus on atmosphere (there's music, the instructors are more inspirational speaker than fitness coaches, and there are candles), it's the narrative that entices people to try it out.

SoulCycle offers a tribal, transcendent experience with each workout:

*"Our riders say it's changing their lives. With every pedal stroke, our minds clear and we connect with our true and best selves. Through this shared SOUL experience, our riders develop an unshakeable bond with one another. Friendships are made and relationships are built. In that dark room, our riders share a Soul experience. We laugh, we cry, we grow — and we do it together, as a community."*

There's the promise of real motivation and a sense of belonging. The high-powered workout almost becomes an afterthought to the excitement of signing up for a SoulCycle cardio party.

## Derma E

A great brand story does you no good if the product you're using it to sell doesn't exceed consumers' expectations. Derma E began with a category-killer product: a naturally derived moisturizing cream that really delivered results. When the brand was established 30 years ago, natural beauty products were fringy, appealing to granola eaters and hemp wearers who were more eco-conscious than self-conscious.

With a great product as a baseline, Derma E built a reputation among vegans — but it wasn't until the brand repositioned itself that it broadened its appeal to younger consumers. That repositioning triggered triple-digit growth in the first two years.

The brand shaped a new narrative that helped consumers connect the dots between ethical, clean beauty products and looking their best. It isn't an either-or. The brand's story links its health-food origins, its unique formulation, its commitment to natural ingredients, and its products' great results:

*"DERMA E didn't start out in the beauty aisle or the boardroom. Instead, we began in a small health food store in Southern California. Our first product was a jar of Vitamin E 12,000 I.U. Moisturizing Cream. People were amazed at the results it had on their skin and word caught on.*

*"Over the years we've introduced many extraordinary products, each one rooted in our belief that skin health can be visibly*

*improved through the right combination of potent vitamins, wholesome nutrients and exceptional ingredients. Today we've grown to become one of the largest natural facial care brands in the U.S. We attribute our success to honoring our customers with products that promote healthier-looking skin and business ethics that promote a healthier world."*

The brand's website is a hub for consumers seeking information and inspiration, with a glossary of key ingredients and their benefits, a blog that spotlights skincare treatments, and, yes, pathway to purchase.

## Reinforcing Consumer Belief

A website allows for the long-form narrative structure that facilitates storytelling. Social media, by contrast, is short, quick, snackable — in fact, social media marketing should always guide the consumer back to the brand website for more and deeper content and purchasing options.

Brand and product stories, communicated in a cohesive visual and verbal style, move consumers from merely transactional encounters to advocacy, from need and want to crave. As the hub of your Brand Ecosystem, your website must reinforce the reasons why your audience believes in you.

## Your Competitive Audit: Website

1.  Does your brand's website have a clear, compelling statement of why your company or brand exists?

2.  Is your website searchable, shop-able, and optimized for mobile?

3. Is it a conversation instead of a brochure? What is the conversation?

4. Do you have an integrated content strategy that makes your website the center of your brand's universe?

5. Could another brand lift your content and erode your share of mind — and, ultimately, market share?

# BELOVED & DOMINANT BRANDS

# Chapter 6

# Direct Marketing: Enchanting Customers by Speaking Only to Them

*figure 6-1: The Brand Ecosystem: Direct Marketing*

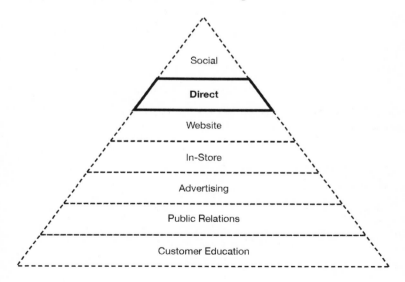

Spend just a few moments browsing the offerings at any online source for promotional items, and you'll bear witness to the history of direct marketing. A whole industry sprung up in the 1990s pitching logoed coffee mugs, beer koozies, stress balls, and related stuff. You may have even received one of these promotional gifts from a company seeking your business, probably packaged in a box with a clever message.

Now, we're not suggesting that you mail out logoed shopping totes. But you do need to completely rethink your perception of direct marketing in the context of the BFY space.

Direct marketing today is built on permission and based in trust. In a world of too much information, consumers are prone to ignore most of what they see flowing through their social feeds, popping up on their web browsers, and loading in apps and You-Tube videos. What's more, they're likely to ignore even the stuff they've signed up for that lands in their inbox. (Look at your email inbox: How many communications that you've subscribed to are lurking there unread after a week or more?)

Beloved & Dominant brands establish such deep relationships with their customers that their direct personal communications are not only accepted, but welcomed, anticipated, and read.

Social media is a digital version of direct mail for the modern marketer: focused, targeted, personalized. We'll unpack social media as the top platform in our Brand Ecosystem pyramid in Chapter 7. But in this chapter, we'll focus our conversation on print communication and on its digital cousins that closely resemble traditional direct mail: email and newsletters.

## The Power of Print in a Digital World

Plenty of prognosticators have been ready to declare that print is dead. A look at the media landscape—with dying magazines, shrinking page counts, and struggling newspapers—may convince you it's true.

---

*"Along this path of technological development, many people have also noticed — or more precisely, missed — the kind of physical interaction that human beings innately crave as part of their basic existence. The end result has been the rediscovery and/or rebirth of older analog technologies that provide some kind of tactile physical experience that a purely digital world has started to remove." — Bob O'Donnell[1]*

---

But look more deeply, and you'll see trends that suggest that people increasingly value analog, physical media as an antidote to the proliferation of screen experiences. In spite of predictions to the contrary, printed books still well outsell ebooks. General music fans, not just audiophile geeks, are driving the rise in popularity of vinyl records. Boutique magazines, narrowly focused on a topic of interest to a passionate group readers and printed on lush paper stock, are thriving even as mass-market publications dwindle.

Why are consumers holding on to print materials when that same information could be delivered more easily — and more cheaply — via digital channels? And, more to the point, how can you as a marketer leverage print media to win fans for your BFY brand?

Print isn't just a nostalgia trip. It has its own power to communicate. Three key reasons:

1. **Print is tangible and tactile.** Ink on paper engages multiple senses: sight, touch, even smell. We're more engaged in a message when we run our fingers over a piece of paper, versus swiping across a hard crystal screen. We spend more time with a printed piece, hold onto it longer.

2. **Print is transparent.** Notice how everything looks great online? But flaws that are easily concealed on-screen can't be hidden in the real world. When we get our hands on an object, we see it for what it is. There's no fakery. And in this age of superficiality, when everything from news reports to social interactions are fraught with inaccuracy and insincerity, realness has currency.

3. **Print conveys quality and trust.** Consumers recognize that it costs money to create a print piece; they subconsciously place a higher value on the communication. Print shows your dedication to your brand and your belief in your product; the mere fact that you've spent to produce a printed piece speaks to your legitimacy. Consumers think, "They've gone to the trouble of printing this thing; they must have confidence in the product."

---

*"In a digitally dominated landscape, physical media products are becoming increasingly rare. Used to disembodied blogs or transient videos, consumers are paying more attention to those paper objects that end up in their hands – they're pausing, lingering, and investigating these (slightly) novel creations. And this tactility is associated with another important quality of print media ... trust."*—
Hook Research[2]

---

## Doing Print? Do it Right.

Print's power lies in its specialness. If you're going to invest in print communications, you need to do it strategically and well, with the right message to the right people.

We're not talking about sending a tri-fold brochure to 10,000 households with children in a 10-state region.

We're talking about identifying a targeted group of consumers — those who've already been introduced to your brand narrative, seen your advertising, perhaps purchased your product in store — and engaging them on a deeper level with the right kind of direct marketing.

The production values of the printed piece must reflect your brand's voice and quality. And the message it contains must be worthy of the production values. It's a physical embodiment of what the consumer expects your brand to be.

Printed communications that are truly special and keyed to the consumer's interests can create deeper engagement. Engaged customers are repeat customers, your most valuable customers. A study by Rosetta of 4,800 U.S. consumers found that engaged customers:

- Buy 90% more frequently
- Spend 60% more per transaction
- Are 5x more likely to say the brand is the only one they'll purchase in the future

# Direct = Speaking Only to That Customer

Here's the thing about the term "direct marketing" — note the word direct. How direct is it to send a letter that reads, "Dear Customer" or a batch of coupons for stuff they'll never buy? Direct communication should be an experience for the customer (and we'll touch more on that in a moment). So I asked Joe Pine, co-author with Jim Gilmore of "The Experience Economy," about how brands of all stripes can use direct communication to create experiences.

*"While in today's Experience Economy stores really must offer time well spent or risk becoming commodity providers (competing with Amazon, Walmart, etc.), they certainly can turn their direct communications into engaging experiences as well,"* he told me.

*"They can embrace our principle to '-ing the thing' — to use gerunds to express the experiencing of their offerings, communications, websites, packaging, etc.*

*"For direct mail and other such communications, I think it's key to focus on customizing. Learn from past interactions across all channels to customize your communications to this individual, living, breathing person, and then learn from that interaction and the next, and so on, and so on, until you cultivate a learning relationship that grows and deepens over time so consumers come to understand how deeply you know them."*

Pine continued with a caution that resonates as consumers grow increasingly wary of sharing TMI with brands. *"Brands must be careful here to at some point go beyond customizing the communications to customizing the actual offerings, lest consumers think you're merely using information to better target them for what you want to sell, rather than discover how you can provide what they want to buy."*

## Old Direct Mail Tactics, New Direct Marketing Tricks

Traditionally, direct mail was a tactic that marketers deployed to capture a prospect's attention before the sale. But, as we'll see in a moment, today's direct marketing can be tailored to someone who's already bought the product.

Direct marketing takes lots of forms: slick Restoration Hardware-style catalogs, cheap postcards, personalized letters, self-mailers, and, yes, logo-embossed beer koozies. So let's hone in on these longstanding direct tactics and explore how marketers can hack them to benefit modern BFY brands.

## Personalized Communication: Coupons and More

According to the Coupon Sherpa, Coca-Cola co-owner Asa Chandler invented the coupon in 1887, using paper "tickets" (which he dubbed "coupons," from the French word couper, to cut) that offered customers a free glass of his new soft drink. Food, beverage, and personal-care brands (as well as retail stores) began offering savings on products via consumers that customers would clip out of newspapers, packages, and magazines. By the mid-1960s, half of all American households used coupons.

Today, paper coupons seems so, well, old-fashioned. But they're alive and well, particularly as grocery retailers seek every possible edge in a hyper-competitive and price-sensitive marketplace.

Other retailers are strategic about delivering relevant content to consumers, using a magazine or magazine-hybrid type of print vehicle. These publications range from mini-catalogs with tons of brand personality like Trader Joe's Fearless Flyer, to small foodie lifestyle publications created by chains large (Publix) and small (Dorothy Lane Markets). These publications are typically distributed in-store; anyone can pick them up. They're a great way to spotlight items and move product.

Backed by data, insight, and technology, coupons and other customized mail can be a high-touch marketing tool for BFY brands. Brands that excel in direct-to-consumer business, like Amazon, are at an advantage in creating personalized printed communications. More to the point, brands with extensive data about their customers — such as REI, The Home Depot, Starbucks, and others — can leverage direct marketing. These brands have a loyal, semi-captive audience and tons of data to garner insights from, so they can create, test, and optimize offers, products, and deals until they find the mix that resonates. In the BFY arena, there are smaller, start-up brands using these tools to quickly generate a revenue stream that gets investors' attention.

## Personalized Communication: Who's Doing it Well?

### Kroger

Nobody does couponing better than Kroger. The country's largest retail grocery chain has even acquired its own marketing agency to turn consumer direct marketing into a highly technical blend of science and art. Armed with deep data about its customers' shopping carts, Kroger has embraced a direct marketing strategy that delivers coupons for products it knows customers have purchased before or will be likely to purchase in the future. Not just packaged and prepared foods — the big brands commonly featured in conventional advertising circulars — but fresh produce, BFY snacks, bakery items, dairy, and more.

As of the article's publication in 2013, Kroger had generated $10 billion in revenue from these highly customized, coupon-based direct marketing efforts.

---

*"Kroger, the Cincinnati-based grocery store chain, calls the 11 million pieces of direct mail it sends to customers each quarter 'snowflakes' — because if any two are the same, it is a fluke. The redemption rate is over 70 percent within six weeks of the mailing."* — Tom Groenfeldt[3]

---

Kroger packages coupons in a couple of ways: as self-mailers with coupons inserted and as part of the brand's MyMagazine consumer publication. As with the coupon program, MyMagazine is highly customized according to consumers' shopping habits, with a tailored mix of articles, recipes, and special offers.

## Packaging as Direct Marketing

Packaging as a direct marketing tactic? You bet. Especially for brands that sell online, either through third parties like Amazon or Whole Foods or direct to consumer. We've covered how packaging works for your brand in the retail environment in Chapter 4. But here, we'll focus on how packaging functions as a key part of the customer experience after you've made the sale.

When consumers order online, the products they've requested show up in their world in decidedly unspectacular fashion. A brown corrugated box, despite the Amazon smiley face on the outside, does not inspire delight. Inside there may be some plastic cushioning ... but really, the product just sort of sits there. There's nothing special about the experience.

Unless the brand has taken care to make the unboxing experience special. As Joe Pine told me, *"Packaging can be a great place to focus. What is your box-opening experience when consumers receive a subscription? How do you design the layering of its contents to create a sense of drama? How can you enhance that first product-trying experience?"*

Unboxing — people opening packages containing stuff they've ordered online, as giddy as if they were unwrapping a gift — is a "thing." One unboxing channel on YouTube has more than 14 million subscribers. Why do people care about the unboxing experience?

"It's a social occasion that partially replaces shopping in bricks and mortar stores. When you can't touch or feel the product unboxing videos provide transparent, human validation and a glimpse at the product in a way that's unmediated by the brand." — Richard Bayston[4]

This is packaging as direct mail: packaging carefully designed using the right materials and graphics to create a sense of delight when it lands in the customer's hands.

Savvy brands across categories are making their direct-to-consumer packaging an inflection point that builds a deeper relationship with consumers. And they're thinking of direct-to-consumer packaging differently than they think about retail packaging. Consumers need something different from you online than at retail. While shopping at Kroger, your prospect can walk down an aisle she's familiar with, she can see a range of products to compare, she can pick up, touch, flip over, read, question, and even go online on her phone to learn more.

The online shopping experience is vastly different. The shopper can't pick up a package to read the ingredients, she's choosing from a visually dissonant gallery of thumbnail images that may or may not accurately represent the products. Her search isn't constrained by what she can see up and down the aisle, but it goes on for pages and pages and pages.

---

*In 2005, two-thirds of shoppers said that their local supermarket was their primary shopping destination, according to the 2016 U.S. Grocery Shopping Trends report from the retail trade group FMI. [In 2016], fewer than half of shoppers do. The hegemony of the supermarket has been broken by the rise of food shopping options, particularly convenience stores, superstores, and online shopping."* — Derek Thompson[5]

---

For BFY brands, especially those designed to address specific nutritional needs or with complex technical attributes, their DTC packaging is an opportunity to reinforce the consumer's decision to buy. A well-crafted box or bag can essentially upsell the product, creating an impression that it's going to taste better and work better because the experience of the packaging is superior. It can set expectations about the product and reassure the buyer, all at once.

Savvy BFY brands recognize that packaging is a reassurance tool, especially for products sold online. They're investing in higher production values, better materials, and a more upscale design aesthetic for DTC packaging that's different from what they sell at Whole Foods or Target.

We're also seeing food brands that supply their top two or three flavors to the brick and mortar retail channel; reserving their broader product line for DTC sales. In a hypercompetitive retail market, it's difficult (or expensive) to land 20 products on shelf at Kroger. Online, the shelf is theoretically limitless, whether you're selling via Amazon or your own platform. Through the DTC channel, brands can better control the consumer experience with their products.

Furthermore, they can get real-time feedback on what's selling and can respond quickly. If you land a product into 700 Kroger stores and it doesn't sell, you've got a problem on your hands; if you're manufacturing just in time for online sales, you can reduce or eliminate the product or retool the keywords and copy on Amazon to attract the right kind of customer.

In the ecommerce space, great packaging creates an opportunity for your brand to have a post-purchase cuddle with the user. She's already bought, so you can take your time communicating with her. Once she's invited you into her home, you're on a first-name basis; she's given your brand permission to say and do more. And she'll give your brand time and attention she won't give a brand in the aisle at Kroger. At the same time, once your brand lands in her home, she'll pay attention to all your other products when she shops in a brick and mortar store.

As Joe Pine told me, *"You can make packaging engaging in the presenting of your product, you can let customers have a reusing experience by, say, turning a big cardboard box into an end table (as one company I know did), or using augmented reality to provide an engaging and informing experience through the consumers phone, as SGK provides for many of its CPG customers."*

## Packaging: Who's Doing it Well?

### Dollar Shave Club

DTC men's grooming brand Dollar Shave Club is hailed for its great packaging, for good reason. It's a compelling example of how Beloved & Dominant brands can build deep relationships with consumers through cardboard and ink. The digital-native brand launched as the most buzzworthy razor company, secured its premium market position with a 2016 deal with Unilever, and is expanding into categories beyond razors and shaving cream.

What's notable about DSC's unboxing experience is that it's so minimal (and an refreshing reminder that packaging doesn't have to be luxurious to wow) — but that minimalism is totally on brand. Once a month, the subscriber, or "member," gets a corrugated box with inserts for a razor and blades. The physical package is simple, with smart copy that speaks directly to the guy using the shared language of the fraternity. The three points of interaction with the brand — the website, the shipping package, and the product — unite to create a killer user experience.

### Digital Direct Mail: Email Newsletters and Promotions

In traditional marketing strategy, direct mail is about the sender not the recipient; it pays little attention to whether the mailing is relevant or welcome.

Today, direct has evolved into an opt in, subscription-based world. This type of direct marketing gives brands the power to engage in conversations with consumers in a longer format and on a more intimate level. It provides the opportunity to tell your brand story in a way that's distinct from other channels.

How often do you visit a website that almost instantly pops up a window inviting you to share your email address in exchange for an alluring discount? Probably never.

There's a reason for that. While it's often neglected by digital marketing teams in a world dominated by the next social media tactic, email marketing remains a tried-and-true avenue for direct-to-consumer marketing — and one that arguably drives better long-term results than other methods. As the retail land-scape becomes more challenging for brands, more companies are turning to online sales and marketing.

1.  In 2017, global email users amounted to 3.7B. This figure is set to grow to 4.3B in 2022 (Statista *a*). How's that for per-spective? Facebook has a little over 2 billion monthly active users, Twitter has 336 million. Email reaches more than 80% of the world's adult population, giving any brand a much wider reach than other channels

2.  The number of emails sent and received per day will rise from 269B in 2017 to 333B in 2022 (Statista *b*). Yes, that's per day! A 23% steady growth rate for a channel that has a deep penetration to begin with is very impressive. As the internet reaches people who have been deprived of it till now, email usage is the one thing that is sure to keep increasing.

3.  Over 90% of consumers use their email at least once every day (Sales Force *c*). The figures might differ slightly based on different studies, but at least 90% seems to be the accepted proportion of daily active users of email. Most people don't just create email accounts and forget about them.

4.  Despite the rise of social messaging apps, 78% of teenagers continue to use email (Adestra *d*). There has been a lot of talk about the rise of social media and instant messaging sounding the death knell for email. Well, according to the set of email statistics linked above, 78% of U.S. teenagers still rely on email. The growth of email usage is driven by millennials and baby boomers alike.

## Direct to Consumer Marketing: Emphasis on the Word CONSUMER

Digital direct marketing is not about you. It's about your customers, about making them feel a part of the tribe surrounding your brand.

Since you're taking the time to get people to engage beyond the deal, this is not the place to be couponing. It's about using relevant content to invite consumers to become part of their narrative. Let's look at a few strategies for leveraging direct digital communications with customers who've granted you permission to stay in touch — and a few brands that are doing it well.

## 1. Put the Brand in Context of a Larger Story

For several years, Alden's Organic Ice Cream has published a customer newsletter, and for a long time, their newsletter strategy was to share pictures of happy people enjoying ice cream on a warm, sunny day. These days, Alden's offers newsletter recipients some value beyond the product. Instead of saying, "Hey, it's hot this July! You should eat tons of vanilla ice cream!" they say, "Here's how to make an ice cream birthday cake from this product."

Then they introduce you to the 40 family farms they've created relationships with to sustain multi-generational organic farming, making consumers feel like do-gooders by association. All they have to do is eat ice cream – tough work, right? Telling this type of deeper story helps the audience feel like they contribute to that family farm. As a result, price no longer becomes an issue.

## 2. Become Part of Customers' Lives

Here in the Pacific Northwest, Alaska Airlines is a major carrier, and it's the airline of choice for folks in our office. (Who doesn't love their tagline, "Fly smart. Land happy"?) One of our team, a VIP member of their Mileage Plan, gets weekly emails from Alaska Airlines. "Their newsletter is always welcome," she says. "They know I live in Seattle and that I have a friend in Sacramento — I know they're stalking me online and I love it because they are helping me prioritize visiting my friend with a great airfare."

Another favorite brand among our team is Outdoor Voices, a brand of workout apparel that's not about poses and performance and perfect muscles, but instead about getting outdoors, being active, and having fun. The brand's mantra is "Doing Things"; they stand for recreation as a way of staying fit, as opposed to spending hours in the gym. Newsletter customers — a community of people committed to fitness — get in on the latest products, inspiration from athletes and artists and everyday people, and special birthday gifts.

## 3. Become a Curator and Guide

Some brands strongly urge or even require consumers to sign up for regular communication — and that means they'd better deliver value for customers if they've gained permission to show up in their inboxes regularly. The home design site Houzz is a great example: The brand combines all the home decor fantasizing and inspiration of Pinterest with access to products and home design services, all in one place. As one Houzz devotee in our office puts it, "It's inspiration and interior design fantasy that takes me out of my everyday." The brand's communication strategy works because it isn't a hard sell; it lures customers in by showing them images of what they could bring into their lives.

Houzz shares editorial-style content and advice, everything from tips on combining decorating styles, home tours, before-and-after project profiles, even a monthly checklist for home maintenance. Using Houzz is like working with an interior decorator who understands your style precisely and is friendly and knowledgeable about making recommendations just for you.

## 4. Solve Customers' Problems

The strategy of offering advice and recommendations plays to another powerful digital direct marketing strategy: Solve their problems. The pet products retailer Chewy can supply pet food via an auto-ship method, so Fido never runs out of kibble. Owners get a reminder a week ahead of time and can change their shipping date to accommodate their needs. (Some subscription-based e-tailers make it difficult for customers to edit their regular orders or alter shipping dates.)

Knowing your customers as well as you do — because they're part of your brand's tribe — you should be able to easily anticipate their problems even before they know they have them. Look for ways you can leverage that data to help them. They'll welcome your direct communication when you solve their problems and save them time.

## Going Old-School

We see a huge opportunity for Beloved & Dominant brands to adopt "old-school" direct marketing in a new way. This includes producing bespoke pieces that have higher production value. Think of versioning and back-end marketing integration that speaks directly to the customer and invites them to have a them-focused conversation about your products and services.

Although direct mail is easy to do, it takes a little bit more effort than social media. However, it gives brands the opportunity to be more intimate and have more meaningful conversations with key consumers. Your brand must take the time to get them involved in why you exist beyond the product.

## Your Competitive Audit: Direct Marketing

1. How are you delivering your brand or product story through each direct marketing touchpoint?

2. In what ways are you helping your audience instead of simply selling to them? What is better about their life because your brand or product exists?

3. What mechanisms are in place to determine how engaged people are beyond promotional pricing, couponing, and special offers? Do people engage beyond the deal?

4. Is communication delivered with your brand's voice?

# Chapter 7

# Social Media: Nurturing a Dialog With Consumers Who Love You

*figure 7-1: The Brand Ecosystem: Social Media*

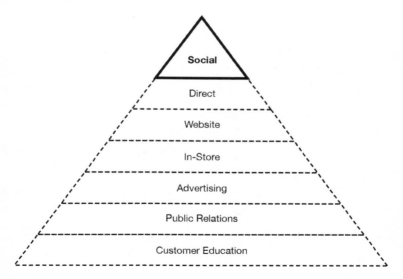

You've built a strong customer education platform that informs and inspires. Traditional and modern media outlets, both online and off, are talking about your brand story and your terrific products. Your messaging is calling out to gather your tribe. Thanks to the strong relationships you've built with retail partners, your in-store experience is engaging and effective. Your website serves as a place where prospects can investigate you and fans can learn more. When customers give you permission to communicate with them, you do it in a way that leaves them wanting more.

Each stage in our Brand Ecosystem builds upon the layers below it. There's a reason why social media is the top tier of the model: When you have everything else in place, social is where the magic happens.

But it's not magic. It's practical, thoughtful, diligent, consistent, strategic.

If you simply jump straight into the social space — perhaps because it seems easy and cheap and fun — without doing the work to layer the other elements beneath it, you have no chance.

- No chance of creating deeply meaningful relationships between your brand and your audience
- No chance of winning fans that crave you with their mind, body, and soul
- No chance in escaping One of Many and becoming Beloved & Dominant

---

More than 40% of digital consumers use social networks to research new brands and products.[a]

---

## Social Media Is the Worst. Social Media Is the Greatest.

This chapter would look very different if it were written a few years ago. Since 2016, social media and tech companies have been taking it on the chin, as users increasingly recognize the perils the platforms pose. Seemingly benign channels for staying in touch with others are harvesting personal data, giving voice to reprehensible people and ideas, reinforcing bias, and sparking depression and anxiety in users. We're both more and less connected than ever.

Our relationship to our devices is similarly paradoxical: We get a dopamine rush when we check the Facebook app on our phone to see how many likes our latest post has garnered, yet we know that so much screen time can't be good for us. Even people who crave the analog experience spend 2+ hours a day on their mobile devices. On average, Americans check their smartphones 52 times per day according to Deloitte's 2018 Global Mobile Consumer Survey. Screens are standing in the way between us and real life.

Even the founder of the World Wide Web, Tim Berners-Lee, acknowledges that the web has become "weaponized" by tech companies, governments, and organizations wielding outsized influence. In 2018, to mark the web's 29th birthday, Berners-Lee posted an open letter on his Web Foundation site outlining the challenges — challenges that early technologists could hardly have forecast.

*"What was once a rich selection of blogs and websites has been compressed under the powerful weight of a few dominant platforms. This concentration of power creates a new set of*

*gatekeepers, allowing a handful of platforms to control which ideas and opinions are seen and shared. ..."*

*"What's more, the fact that power is concentrated among so few companies has made it possible to weaponize the web at scale. In recent years, we've seen conspiracy theories trend on social media platforms, fake Twitter and Facebook accounts stoke social tensions, external actors interfere in elections, and criminals steal troves of personal data."* — Sir Tim Berners-Lee[1]

In this era of the weaponized web, consumers are becoming rightfully wary and distrustful. Legitimate communication is labeled fake, false information is taken for truth, and no one knows what to believe anymore.

The word "authentic" is wildly overused, and yet it represents a brand's path to success in this social media environment. Beloved & Dominant brands are relentlessly, obsessively true to their missions — their WHY — especially on social media.

A brand's ethos — the way it behaves in the world — has to be unwaveringly consistent across all channels. When a consumer experiences the brand in an unexpected way (say, for example, the tone of the brand's website is warm and inviting but its social posts are snarky, or its mission embraces environmental sustainability but its packaging isn't recycled), the consumer starts to question her assumptions about the brand. Those questions likely direct her dollars to a competitor.

*"Brands succeed when they break through in culture. And branding is a set of techniques designed to generate cultural relevance. Digital technologies have not only created potent new social networks but also dramatically altered how culture works. Digital crowds now serve as very effective and prolific innovators of culture — a phenomenon I call crowdculture."* — Douglas Holt[2]

## Reaching the Right Consumers Through the Right Platforms

For all their similarities, social media platforms have settled into well-defined patterns of usage:

LinkedIn = head
Facebook = heart
Instagram = soul
Twitter = mouth

LinkedIn is a business and professional outlet primarily related to employment: recruiting job candidates and proving your expertise. Facebook allows users to talk to people who they already know, join groups of like-minded folks, and follow brands they like. Twitter functions as a soapbox.

For marketers, Instagram is where it's at; it's entirely visual and skews to a younger demographic. Instagram feels "real" to millennials.

For Gen Z and younger millennials, social media carries greater influence over the brands they try and buy than conventional advertising. These consumers are hungry for social proof: Because they want to be accepted by others, they mimic the choices they see among the peer group they aspire to. Recommendations and referrals for products they view as they're scrolling through their Instagram feeds influence their own behavior and decision-making. Monkey see, monkey do. "I won't buy a brand at the grocery store unless I've seen it on my friend's Instagram, because I don't want to be embarrassed by picking the wrong facial scrub or sandal or trail mix," they think.

What's more, Gen Z and younger millennials have, on average, five screens in their lives (including TV, laptop, mobile devices), and they move fluidly from one to the next. They multitask with ease; they monitor multiple social media sites, do work, listen to music, and instant message with friends — all at the same time, on different devices running different apps.

Beloved & Dominant brands use the instantaneous, short-attention-span nature of social media to their advantage by making their social communication so smart and snackable that users who care about the brand will share it and provide social proof to their sphere of influence.

And that — creating innately sharable content that reaches beyond fans to their connections — is the value of social media to a brand.

---

Social media drives 3x more traffic for non-customers than customers.[b]

---

## The Art of Social Media

Brands simply can't overlook social marketing. Your competitors are operating in that space already, and if you want to stand out, your social strategy has to be steeped in your brand story, shared through visuals and language that translates your brand positioning, and executed with a plan that favors consistency.

There is a straight line running from customer education to social media. When you know what kind of educator you are and who makes up your audience, you can talk about your ethos and your products in ways that are different and meaningful and appealing to the tribe, no matter the platform. Yes, you need people to like and share your brand — but the bigger goal of social marketing is to use your education platform to get people to make your brand part of their lives.

Beloved & Dominant brands recognize the difference between social advertising (one way from brand to consumer) and social marketing (a dialog between brand and consumer). They use social channels for conversation, not promotion. They lean on their customer education platform for content that they share in a voice and language that's consistent and common to the tribe.

---

Gen Y and millennial consumers consider social media to be the advertising channel most relevant to them.[c]

---

The truth is that consumers have little interest in the content that ordinary brands churn out. Most of that content is strictly promotional, branded messaging. Most people consider it essentially spam, even if they have liked your brand. They'll tune out content that smacks of advertising. Just because consumers have granted you access to be part of their lives on social media does not mean that they've granted you permission to sell to them. At most, 10% of your messaging should have any kind of sales component; the rest of your content should be about something else.

---

Just because consumers have granted you access to be part of their lives on social media does not mean that they've granted you permission to sell to them.

---

In real time, social media marketing should look fluid and spontaneous. And your strategy, even though it's considered and planned, should allow for that fluidity and spontaneity. The brand needs to operate as part of its community, sharing and engaging with fans in the moment. And because it's part of the tribe, the brand should know its audience — who they are, what they respond to, what they love, what they struggle with — so well that the content you produce will automatically capture their attention.

## Show How Your Product Fits into Your Audience's Lives

We often see brands aligning their product with too many lifestyles – diluting their message and lacking consistent storytelling. However, success stems from focusing in on a specific, targeted audience. Instead of showing your product simply existing in a lifestyle, share how it lives and fits within that lifestyle.

When a brand reaches Beloved & Dominant status, its products become fully intertwined in its customers' lives. Remember the Customer Journey map: Beyond adoption lies belonging and advocacy. Once the customer has made several purchases and leans into fandom, she starts to feel like she's part of something bigger that the brand makes possible for her. The brand aligns with her self-identity. It's part of her world.

Social media allows marketers to reach these superfans, to connect them with others, to surround them with meaning, and to show how the brand embraces them. It's lifestyle-oriented marketing, yes, but the strategy goes deeper than that.

Humans are hardwired to look for patterns, danger, and pleasure (according to Sigmund Freud) and so we see them in everything. When a brand knows its WHY, creates a specific educator profile, and acknowledges its tribe of followers as special, it has the opportunity to leverage human nature much more rapidly, deeply, and meaningfully than brands who simply use social as a marketing channel. Social media is the ideal space for story creation, and brands build profound connections when their stories echo and repeat patterns that are identifiable and irresistible to their tribes.

*"Anthropologists tell us that storytelling is central to human existence. That it's common to every known culture. That it involves a symbiotic exchange between teller and listener – an exchange we learn to negotiate in infancy.*

*"Just as the brain detects patterns in the visual forms of nature – a face, a figure, a flower – and in sound, so too it detects patterns in information. Stories are recognizable patterns, and in those patterns we find meaning. We use stories to make sense of ourworld and to share that understanding with others. They are the signal within the noise.*

*"So Powerful is our impulse to detect story patterns that we see them even when they're not there" - Frank Rose[3]*

## Don't Just Talk; Listen

With the rise of social media, consumers now have a direct line to companies whose products and services they purchase. They can use social media to share their love or hate for a product, discuss price point, and even provide suggestions for taste, formula, or design. The feedback BFY brand can get on social media is a goldmine for product, marketing, sales, and executive management.

As we mentioned, Beloved & Dominant brands use social for two-way communication, and they value the opportunity for social listening. In fact, it's the only way — short of holding focus groups — to listen to your consumers. On social networks, brand marketers can interact and participate with consumers to understand their hopes, fears, ambitions, and what they get tired of.

Social listening, coupled with your own consumer data, can add perspective and qualitative intel to what's otherwise quantitative, historical insight. What can you learn that's actionable? As a marketer, you automatically get more deeply in touch with the biorhythm of their days, weeks, and years. You start to become part of their world as they are part of yours; together, you're able to create a shared culture (or a better version of your culture).

Social engagement is not just about creating attraction and generating likes. It's about actively listening, then reflecting back to them what you hear in a way that makes your audience think, "They like me, they listen to me, they know me, they understand me." That's what cult brands are all about.

That's when co-authoring and advocacy happens. When the consumer hears her own input in your offering, she won't be able to resist it and will advocate for you. When you're agile and adaptive and can incorporate her ideas, you move from One of Many to Beloved & Dominant. It really is that simple.

Reflective listening on social media works as well for giant multinational brands as it does for niche indies. What we're talking about here does not require tons of money; rather, it requires time and emotional intelligence and a willingness to listen. Importantly, whoever is managing your social communication has to be part of the community, speak the lingo, share the passion. (In fact, that's why we develop social strategies for our clients, but we don't manage the posting. Social is powerful when the posts come from a staffer who's part of the tribe.) They can use the right brand voice, they know the competitive set, they're emotionally engaged, and they're essentially speaking to their peers and friends.

## One Caveat on Social Media

More than any other marketing channel, social has low bar to entry; there's zero cost for setting up a brand account and for posting, and low cost for content creation and for hiring young marketing assistants. Because it's cheap and easy, brands often haphazardly throw stuff out on social media.

Brands fail to have a successful social media presence when their content isn't ownable. In other words, when they lack a point of view or a unique tone of voice. It doesn't become ownable unless it ladders up to your WHY. Your social content should be so credible, relevant, authentic, and believable that your audience knows it comes from your brand without them having to see your logo.

That's our benchmark for Beloved & Dominant brands: We'll swap out the logo and see how ownable social communication is. If you can replace the brand's logo with any of its competitors', then the content lacks originality and won't stand out to consumers.

## Social Media: Who's Doing it Well?

To search for brands that are rocking social media marketing, one only need look to the growing cohort of brands built on, for, and by social platforms. These brands invite consumers to learn, commune, and buy — all without ever leaving Instagram.

## The Good Patch

The Good Patch is a product from La Mend that delivers CBD infusions through a patch applied to the skin. With all the buzz and confusion surrounding CBD and an atypical delivery method, the brand has a lot of educating and confidence-building to do. For BFY brands marketing products with technical ingredients or functional benefits, social media is the ideal channel to help consumers understand how and when to use those products.

The Good Patch's Instagram feed checks off all the boxes: a strong educator profile (the wise friend), a consistent visual strategy (all the millennial pastels), and the right mix of inspiration and information.

## Dr. Jart

Ceramides. Tiger Grass. Antioxidants. Natural skincare is increasingly complex. The Dr. Jart brand is positioned on the intersection of science and art in skincare, and its social profile and website lean heavily on the art. The digital-native brand was cofounded by a Korean dermatologist and an architect in 2005, before the Korean beauty craze swept the U.S. The brand's packaging looks clinical but with pops of color, and that color drives its social marketing.

Dr. Jart leverages the power of social media in an age of social proof — consumers need to see their friends embracing a product before they try it themselves. Its Instagram feed is totally on-brand, and it prompts lots of "ooh ... I have to try this" comments.

## Build Competitor-Proof Relationships with Customers

Consumers are increasingly skeptical of the power they grant social channels in their lives, even as they still willingly give that power.

Because of the rapid pace of life and the amount of information that floods us everywhere, people say they don't want brands in their social spheres. But all of us use brands to shape our social selves and personal identities in the way that previous generations used universities, social clubs, family ties, and religion. Brands are institutions we align ourselves with. And when consumers think of brands as part of their social sphere, they're willing to open their social channels to those brands.

When a brand has gained that trust and access, it had better behave honorably and honestly. If you don't get social marketing right, you're just another product. Engage in an authentic way with the people who've invited you into their lives, and they'll go to bat for you every time. Even when other brands come into the space, they'll retain a strong preference for you. If you're part of their consideration set — even if they don't choose your product every single time — you'll secure Beloved & Dominant status.

## Your Competitive Audit: Social Media

1. What evidence do you have to support your claim that you are different than your competition?

2. Do you have a unique tone and voice?

3. Can you describe your brand's unique tone and voice by reading your social media posts?

4. Are you a lifestyle brand instead of merely a product? How does your social media prove this?

# Conclusion

# The Tip of the Brand Ecosystem Iceberg

So, you've got a strong educational platform that informs and inspires both fans and newcomers to your brand. Respected, influential people are talking about your brand and products. You're sharing your message in a way that calls to your tribe. You've developed a great in-store experience through supportive retail relationships. Your website works as a place where people can investigate your promise. When you've gained permission to communicate with your audience — via email, coupons, packaging, or social media — you delight and engage them at every turn.

Everything — all the guidance in this book — is predicated on the fact that the brand knows its WHY.

Beloved & Dominant brands pursue robust marketing strategies that encompass education and retail and social media and the rest of the seven Brand Ecosystem components. The strategies that we've outlined are essential to winning fans who crave your brand with mind, body, and soul. That's the **beloved** part of the equation.

Category **dominance** comes from having a sound brand strategy that underpins the marketing strategy.

The Brand Ecosystem represents the tip of the proverbial iceberg; these are the **marketing touchpoints** at which consumers learn about, choose, interact with, and talk about your brand and products. What lies beneath involves heavy-duty brand strategy, organizational development, and audience segmentation. Together, we call this the Brand Quadramid.

## The Brand Quadramid

*figure C-1 The Brand Quadramid showing the Brand Ecosystem as the tip of the brand iceberg*

Executing the brand's marketing touchpoints well will take you far — but doing so on top of a solid strategic foundation will last forever.

---

Brand = the promises you make and the way you keep them.

---

Brand strategy is the throughline that makes the marketing work easier. It removes individual bias and groupthink from the decision-making process. It creates a voice that transcends any individual marketing message or advertising campaign. It shines a bright light on opportunity, because the brand's path into the future is easy to follow.

## What Does Beloved & Dominant Look Like?

Imagine your brand's future state — when you've built a seven-point marketing strategy on top of a bold WHY. What might success look like?

- You've secured preferential status for your brand and your products to your most critical audiences, both internal and external
- People fall in love with your brand and talk about it
- You command a premium price in the category
- You've gone beyond competing on features and benefits
- You've become the defining example of your category — your brand has become a verb, like FedExing or Googling. Joe Pine, coauthor of "The Experience Economy," calls this "ING-ing the thing."
- You've changed the sales process forever; you no longer have to knock on the retailer's door to ask, "Can we get in?" Rather they come to you and ask, "What else you got?"
- Your earned media has increased exponentially
- Your brand has tons of influence on popular culture
- You've become an icon

What's more, the brand's business success has significant personal implications:

- If you're a marketer, this makes your career
- If you're a product innovator, you'll go on to rock stardom

• If you're an investor, your next BFY brand deal is easier

Fame, history, and glory all hang in the balance.

And they're within reach. Take time to answer the questions that wrap up each chapter. Discuss them with your leadership team. Have an honest dialogue about your brand's WHY. Use these chapters — the seven platforms in the Brand Ecosystem — to benchmark your marketing activities against the best in your category, and then against other brands that compete for your customer's time and money.

Do all this with the goal of creating a road map that leads your brand from One of Many to Beloved & Dominant.

# Notes

## Introduction: The Life Cycle of Better-for-you Brands

*Figure I-1:* The Typical Pathway of a Pioneering Brand. Based upon the theory that any invention that is not patented that catches on with a group of core users will, eventually be copied by other manufacturers and brands. Resulting in a once beloved brand being relegated to one of many status.

*Figure I-2:* The Pathway From One of Many to Category Prominence. Based upon *Figure I-1,* shows the pathway of using *the* competitive audit to elevate the brand from competing in a sea of samenss to enjoying category prominence (a.k.a. Beloved & Dominant status).

A Brand is the gut feeling an individual has when they think, see, or hear a brand name based upon a series of promises that organization, company, and/or product has made (whether expressly to them or in general) and the way that person feels about the manner in which the organization, company and/or product has kept said promises.

*Figure I-3* The Brand Ecosystem illustrated as a pyramid.

*Figure I-4* The Brand Ecosystem Unbalanced. Illustrated as a *pyramid* when the marketing components are out of balance. The theory is simple, an unbalanced pyramid will be shaky at best and will not stand up to adversity at all. Ever play Jenga?

# Chapter 1: Customer Education: Turning Buyer Into Believers

*Figure 1-1* The Brand Ecosystem. Illustrated pyramid highlighting Customer Education.

*Figure 1-2* Customer Journey Map showcasing where traditional marketing maps become extended and brands have an opportunity to create advocates through the power of providing loyalists the brand education to evangelize on the brand's behalf.

*Figure 1-3* Brand Ecosystem Unbalanced. When customer education is treated like an after-thought, a list of features and benefits without any reason to believe, or worse, a brand attempting to gain maximum benefit from any other plank in the ecosystem putting their will investment of energy, capital and other resources at risk.

*Figure 1-4* West Marine "Tone & Voice Framework" (2010). Using tone and voice to demonstrate the power of understanding audience segmentation.

1. William Craig, President of WebFX "Don't Market To Your Customers, Educate Them Instead" Forbes.com (2015)

2. Taylor Landis, "Customer Retention Marketing vs. Customer Acquisition Marketing" Outboundengine.com (2019)

3. Simon Sinek, *Start With WHY: How Great Leaders Inspire Everyone to Take Action (*London; Penguin Books Ltd. 2009)

4. B. Joseph Pine and James Gilmore *The Experience Economy: Work Is Theater & Every Business a Stage (*Boston, Harvard Business Press, 1999)

5. Jung, C.G. *Archetypes and the Collective Unconscious Collected Works of C.G. Jung, Volume 9 (Part 1)*, (Princeton, N.J.: Princeton University Press, 1969)

6. Clifford Geertz *The Interpretation of Cultures: Selected Essays,* (Chicago, Basic Books 1973). Geertz's definition of World View outlines culture as "a system of inherited conceptions expressed in symbolic forms by means of which men communicate, perpetuate, and develop their knowledge about and attitudes toward life."

7. Whole Foods "Whole Story Blog" (2019)

8. Monterey Bay Aquarium Seafood Watch, founded in 1999 is one of the best known sustainable seafood advisory lists, and has influenced similar programs around the world. It is best known for developing science-based seafood recommendations that consumers, chefs, and business professionals use to inform their seafood purchasing decisions. https://www.seafoodwatch.org/

# Chapter 2: Building a Sphere of Authenticity

*Figure 2-1* The Brand Ecosystem, Public Relations

1. Interview with Chris Olivier, Partner of Craft Catalyst May 2019 *"As the disciplines of marketing continue to merge, what role does PR play in building a brand people truly love? What has historically been the point of PR?*

*Generating awareness – public relations is an antiquated term – it has left the original goal in the dust. Today PR is an authenticity play – if it's done correctly becomes third party validation via an unbiased POV from a person with no skin in the game. PR can be monetized. That's the beauty of the PR, Amazon, one-two punch."*

2. Jessica Wohl, "Earned Media is as Important as TV or Events" AdAge (2017)

3. "Lesser Evil Brand Manifesto" January 2019

4. Krista Garver, "Innovation, Collaboration, and the Art of Listening to Your Customers: A Model for Success from Califia Farms founder-owner Greg Steltenpohl" Process Expo (2018)

# Chapter 3: Advertising: Inviting the Right People Into the Tribe

*Figure 3-1* The Brand Ecosystem, Advertising. Advertising is expensive. And losing its relevance to those brands which are able to call to the deep within their tribe of likeminded consumers. Advertising is what you do when everything has been built and you want to step on the gas.

John Wanamaker (July 11, 1838 – December 12, 1922) was an American merchant and a religious, civic political figure, considered by some to be a proponent of advertising and a pioneer in marketing.

# Notes

Insider Baseball: According to Merriam-Webster, the term Insider Baseball originated in the 1890s referring to a particular style of playing the game which relied on singles, walks, bunts, and stolen bases rather than power hitting. Within a few decades the term was being used to mean highly specialized knowledge about baseball, and by the 1950s it was being applied to politics and now refers to details about a subject that require such a specific knowledge about what is being discussed that the nuances are not understood or appreciated by outsiders.

The Dog Whistle came from Edward M. Lambert, former MacKenize super guru and CEO Del Taco.

1. Jessica Wohl, "How Halo Top is Conquering the Ice Cream Biz Without Advertising" AdAge (2017)

2. Ciara Linnane, "Nike's online sales jumped 31% after company unveiled Kaepernick campaign, data show" MarketWatch (2018). "There was speculation that the Nike/Kaepernick campaign would lead to a drop in sales, but the data over does not support that theory."

3. Interview with B. Joseph Pine, Author of *The Experience Economy: Work Is Theater & Every Business a Stage,* (April 2019) *"Well, in far too many cases advertising just gets in the way of great experiences! I mean that pretty literally, as the very nature of advertising is that it interrupts what a person is truly trying to do. That's one reason why I counsel brands to stop advertising. (Other reasons include that it is a phoniness-generating machine, and that it is corrosive to companies for whom it is their lifeblood.) Instead (and again), put your money into demand-generating*

*experiences that entice and engage potential customers
for minutes or hours instead of seconds, that garners their
undivided attention, that has an intensity far greater than
any advertisement can, and yields memorability far greater
than can be measured by recall rate.*

*It's not that advertising can't be engaging -- the best of it
most certainly is -- and there are good reasons to employ
when you need to reach a lot of people about new products,
new positionings, moving into a new geographic area, etc.
But even when it is great and engaging advertising, it still
is interrupting people and can't hold a candle to the other
benefits from experiences."*

# Chapter 4: In-store: Whispering in The Shopper's Ear

*Figure 4-1* The brand Ecosystem, In-store

1. Think With Google "Being There In Micro-moments, Especially On Mobile" (2015)

2. Kat Simpson "How to Translate Brand Strategy Outcomes Into Shelf Science" Retail Voodoo Blog (2019)

3. Interview with Joe Pine, Author of The Experience Economy: Work Is Theater & Every Business a Stage (April 2019) *"I always recommend – get thee into retail! Create an experiential retail outlet that exposes potential customers to your offerings, knowing that if you get customers to experience your offerings before they buy them, the chances they will buy them go up! The idea, as with the original*

*Niketowns, is not to compete with your channel but to increase the pie so that everyone benefits. Gut your advertising budget and put that money into demand-generating experiences that will have much greater ROI and, if you're so good you can charge admission fees for experiences within the place (as scores of brands now do), you could even turn marketing into a profit center.*

*I also recommend you-ing your packaging placed in other channels. Turn your packaging itself into an experience! You can make it engaging in the presenting of your product, you can let customers have a reusing experience by, say, turning a big cardboard box into an end table (as one company I know did), or using augmented reality to provide an engaging and informing experience through the consumers phone, as SGK provides for many of its CPG customers."*

4. Interview with REI's Chief Customer Officer Ben Steele (May 2019) *"The REI store is organized around the relationship with the members... the people who shop and the people who work share the same values."*

*"It's a flywheel.... It's a feeling you get when you walk into the store...and it has been that way since I was growing up in Idaho... and I remember when the store showed up in Boise...it was a big deal because it was a place to go and hear stories from locals who loved the outdoors as much as me and it truly inspired my lifelong love of the outdoors."*

*"The store design was ahead of its time. That we got there ahead of the curve is amazing. A store dedicated to --- store is the wrong word—it's a community space. A lot of the time*

*I find myself feeling blown away at the vision of, the history of, the founding members and the subsequent leadership in the coop – that they were so ahead of trends and gave us a such a tailwind... our job is to uncover and illuminate their original vision, celebrate their courage and commitment to building our community of outdoor advocates."*

*"It's not easy to be this committed... it leaves fewer dollar that a modern organization wants to have at its disposal to achieve modern marketing goals. But its working so well. I am so proud of my team."*

## Chapter 5: Website: Creating the Hub of Your Brand's Storytelling Universe

*Figure 5-1* Brand Ecosystem, Website

1. Julie Krueger "3 mindset shifts CPG marketers should adopt to win today's shoppers" Think With Google (2018)

2. Think With Google, "How mobile has redefined the consumer decision journey for shoppers" (2016)

3. Interview with Ben Steele, REI Chief Customer Officer, May, 2019 *"Some of the best brand work we have ever done has nothing to do with the products we sell. It has everything to do with capturing the power that the outdoors has to improve and inspire people's lives."*

*"Mutual value and relationship and frankly respect is where I think consumers want to put their time and attention.. I can get something from a lot of places but I cannot get more... the value of what I get from the relationship and*

*ability to make me a better version of myself is what people crave more than the 20% off...even though that 20% off is also important...it's not the brand. If you are more than just the 20% off, but also the place I go to learn, to be inspired, to be challenged about my life and my passions, then you (as a brand) are unreplaceable, everyday."*

4. Harrison Monarth "The Irresistible Power of Storytelling as a Strategic Business Tool" Harvard Business Review (2014)

5. Dan McAdams, PhD, "The Stories We Live By: Personal Myths and the Making of the Self" New York (Guilford Publications, 1993)

6. Celinne Da Costa,"Why Every Business Needs Powerful Storytelling to Grow," Forbes (2017)

7. Jung, C.G. *Archetypes and the Collective Unconscious Collected Works of C.G. Jung, Volume 9 (Part 1)*, (Princeton, N.J.: Princeton University Press, 1969)

# Chapter 6: Direct Marketing: Enchanting Customers by Speaking Only to Them

*Figure 6-1* Brand Ecosystem, Direct

Study by Publicis Group Experience Agency, Rosetta (now Publicis Sapient), provide evidence that highly engaged customers have a personal connection to a brand, built on experiences that drive affinity with its ethos. Highly engaged customers recognize when a brand understands their personal needs. They believe that the brand reflects their personal identity – both how they see themselves and how they want others to see them.

1.  Bob O'Donnell, "We're Living in a Digital World but Analog Is Making a Comeback," Vox (2017)

2.  Hook Research, "Trust & Tactility: The Power of Print in a Digital World" (2108)

3.  Why Engaged Customers are Your Best Customers: Facts & Figures on the Value of Engagement

4.  Interview with Joe Pine, co-author of The Experience Economy: Work Is Theater & Every Business a Stage (April 2019) *"I think the goal should be not to provide repeatable experiences but to repeatably provide fresh experiences! Make the interactions different every time, which can be done again through customizing, or through a dramatic arc that encompasses many interactions, or fresh content, and so forth. Do recognize that many customers may very well want the nice/ easy/convenience of time well saved when making replacement purchases, but entice them to go deeper in engaging with the brand when they do have time."*

5.  Tom Groenfeldt, "Kroger Knows Your Shopping Patterns Better Than You Do:" Forbes (2013)

6.  Odoro Blog, "What Can We Learn About the Best Unboxing Experiences?" (2016)

7.  Derek Thompson, "Why Do Millennials Hate Groceries?" The Atlantic (2016)

8.  Corinne Ruff, "Dollar Shave Club expands products amid lifestyle push" Retail Dive (2019)

## Chapter 7: Social Media: Nurturing a Dialog with Consumers Who Love You

*Figure 7-1* The Brand Ecosystem, Social Media

1.  Global mobile consumer survey: US edition "A New Era In Mobile Continues" Deloitte (2018)

2.  Adobe Digital Insights Report (2018). *Based on over 183 billion visits to U.S. Online video data based on 12 billion plays of TVE & 9 billion ad impressions, E-mail analysis based on 150 billion e-mails sent via Adobe Campaign in 2017. With insights ranging from personalization, to relevant ad channels, and how one size does not fit all for video completions.*

3.  Douglas Holt, "The Principles of Cultural Branding" Harvard Busienss Review. (2016). *Social media was supposed to allow your company to leapfrog traditional media and forge relationships directly with customers. If you told them great stories and connected with them in real time, your brand would become a hub for a community of consumers. Businesses have invested billions pursuing this vision. Yet few brands have generated meaningful consumer interest online. In fact, social media seems to have made brands less significant.*

4.  Frank Rose, "The Art of Immersion: Why Do We Tell Stories?" Wired (2011)

# Conclusion: The Tip of the Brand Ecosystem Iceberg

*Figure C-1* The Brand Quadramid illustrating the Brand Ecosystem as above the waterline or the tip of the branding iceberg. The subject of my next book.

# Index